From the **Free Academy** *to* **CUNY**

FROM THE Free Academy

To CUNY

Illustrating Public Higher Education in New York City, 1847–1997

Sandra Shoiock Roff

Anthony M. Cucchiara

Barbara J. Dunlap

FORDHAM UNIVERSITY PRESS
New York
2000

Copyright © 2000 by Fordham University Press

All rights reserved. No part of this publication may be reproduced, stored in a retrieval system, or transmitted in any form or by any means—electronic, mechanical, photocopy, recording, or any other—except for brief quotations in printed reviews, without the prior permission of the publisher.

Every effort has been made to locate and contact owners of copyright for materials used. The authors and the publisher would be grateful to learn of any errors or omissions.

Library of Congress Cataloging-in-Publication Data

Roff, Sandra Shoiock.
    From the Free Academy to CUNY : illustrating public higher education in New York City, 1847–1997 / Sandra Shoiock Roff, Anthony M. Cucchiara, Barbara J. Dunlap.
       p. cm.
    Includes bibliographical references (p.) and index.
    ISBN 0-8232-2019-2—ISBN 0-8232-2020-6 (pbk.)
    1. City University of New York—History. 2. Education, Higher—New York (State)—New York—History.
I.Cucchiara, Anthony M. II. Dunlap, Barbara J. III. Title.

LD3835 .R64 2000
378.747'1—dc21   00-020506

ISBN 0-8232-2019-2 (hc), 0-8232-2020-6 (pbk)

Printed in the United States of America

00 01 02 03 04   5 4 3 2 1

First Edition

Contents

	Preface	vii
1	Establishing Public Higher Education in New York City: From the Free Academy to CCNY, 1846–1913	1
2	Women Enter onto the Scene	22
3	Opportunity Grows with the City	36
4	Student Life at "Subway Schools"	54
5	Student Publications and Journalism	70
6	A Call to Action: City University at War	79
7	Athletics	97
8	Access and Excellence: 1960–1997	111
	Afterword	131
	Bibliography	133
	Websites and Addresses of CUNY Colleges	139
	A Sampling of CUNY Alumni	141
	Index	143

Preface

An anniversary is a classic occasion for reflection. When the anniversary is that of an institution, this landmark date can serve as a time to review its past as well as to survey the artifacts that remain to illustrate its story as it prepares for its future.

For the City University of New York (CUNY), such a recent landmark date was May 7, 1997, the 150th anniversary of the passage and signing of the legislation that created the Free Academy of New York. The United States celebrated Charter Day by issuing a commemorative post card; the city celebrated with a party at Gracie Mansion. Even the Empire State Building was illuminated with City College's colors.

The genesis of this book is the exhibit "From the Free Academy to CUNY: 1847–1997," which opened at Baruch College on the anniversary of Charter Day and celebrated the rich history of the university through text, images, and artifacts. The Free Academy, which was soon renamed the College of the City of New York, and its slightly younger sister, the Normal College (later Hunter College), are the strong foundations upon which the City University of New York was built. Today, eighteen campuses are dispersed throughout New York City's five boroughs, meeting the higher education needs of a diverse student population ranging from community college students to those working toward doctoral or professional degrees. Life in New York City has been greatly enriched by the opportunities provided by the City University of New York over the years.

Many stories emerge from the history of this 150-year experiment. Above all, there is the story of the students, often from poor families, who received the benefits of public higher education in New York City and who, as alumni/ae, have made their mark in all professions and contributed immeasurably to the city, the state, the nation, and the world. There is the story of the faculty, many of them renowned scholars, who inspired and nourished hungry minds in the classroom. There is also the story of the development of a system, which began with a president and a few instructors and grew to be a major university with a chancellor, college presidents, law and medical school deans, and thousands of full- and part-time faculty and staff members. There is even a story about architecture, as the small Gothic Revival building on 23rd Street was replaced and campuses throughout the city were built in a variety of architectural styles.

Like the anniversary exhibit on which it is based, this book narrates in broad terms the growth and development of municipal higher education in New York City. It tells the story of the university's many activities both inside and outside of the classroom over fifteen decades. Although space constraints preclude a detailed discussion of each college and school, at least one aspect of the life of each facility is represented.

Controversy surrounded the establishment of the Free Academy in 1847 and has surfaced many times since, generated by changing economic, political, and social issues. Nevertheless, CUNY has met the needs of thousands of students with varied backgrounds and accomplishments who have depended on public education in New York City to satisfy their desire for knowledge and drive to succeed. Today, the City University of New York is educating more than 200,000 students and continues to evolve. The civic, professional, and cultural life in New York City would be less vibrant without the contributions of the university's alumni/ae. Today's graduates will continue this tradition by contributing to the successes of tomorrow.

We hope that this volume, through its text and illustrations, will illuminate the path that led from the Free Academy to CUNY and, through its documentation, will acquaint historians with the rich array of published and unpublished sources available to them. S. Willis Rudy's *The College of the City of New York, 1847–1947: A Centennial History* sets a high standard for books about the CUNY colleges. Selma Berrol's *Getting Down to Business* continues this tradition as it narrates the complex route leading from the once-slighted "commercial course" to the robust institution that is Baruch College today. These books drew heavily on the archival materials available on the campuses, and we urge new generations of scholars and students to explore the richness of CUNY's history through the many campus archives. Every campus merits a scholarly study of its creation, development, and accomplishments.

The exhibit "From the Free Academy to CUNY: 1847–1997" was supported with grants from the PSC-CUNY Research Foundation, the H. W. Wilson Foundation, the Office of the Chancellor, and the Baruch College Fund, as well as by the presidents of the individual colleges of the City University of New York. Kate Hixon and her designers contributed countless hours to the project, creating a magnificent series of panels that combined text and photographs and exhibiting artifacts to their best advantage in specially designed cases. After its opening at Baruch College on May 7, 1997, the exhibit traveled to several campuses of CUNY.

Support for this publication was provided by a challenge grant offered by Interim Chancellor Christoph M. Kimmich, a grant from the PSC-CUNY Research Foundation, and grants made by former Interim President Lois S. Cronholm (Baruch College), former President Yolanda T. Moses (City College), and President Vernon Lattin (Brooklyn College). This book was made possible through the cooperation, assistance, and suggestions of CUNY archivists: Julio Hernando-Delgado at Hunter College, Janet Butler Munch at Lehman College, Kenneth Riccardi at LaGuardia Community College, Evelyn Hisz at the Borough of Manhattan Community College, Maxine Genn at Queensborough Community College, and Jay K. Williams at the Central Office Archives, as well as Catherine Tyler Brody, Professor Emerita at New York City Technical College and Sidney VanNort, Adjunct Archivist at City College. We would also like to thank Pamela Gillespie, Chief Librarian at City College; Arthur Downing, Chief Librarian at Baruch College; Barbra Higginbotham, Chief Librarian at Brooklyn College; and J. Kevin Barry and Robert Machalow at York College; as well as Terrence Harris of the Special Programs at John Jay College, Margaret Leland Smith of the Criminal Justice Ethics Program at John Jay College, Elizabeth Arcuri of the City University Office of Facilities Planning, Joseph Schenck of Special Events at Queens College, and the many administrators at the campuses of the City University of New York. Support from the Baruch College Fund provided for the excellent editorial assistance of Amy Goldstein. Our thanks also go to Barbara Malczak of Fordham University Press for her editorial guidance.

From the **Free Academy** *to* **CUNY**

1 Establishing Public Higher Education in New York City: From the Free Academy to CCNY, 1847–1913

In 1846, New York City—consisting of Manhattan and some outlying islands—was the busiest port on the eastern seaboard. The masts of tall ships crowded its harbors on the Hudson and East Rivers. More than 450,000 people lived in Manhattan, and soon the famine in Ireland and the political unrest in Europe would bring many more. City functionaries included ballast masters and inspectors of pressed and baled hay, carts, and firewood, and there were 131 licensed keepers of junk shops.[1]

The five-year span before and after 1846 also saw the creation of a number of institutions vital to the city's future. "An Act to establish and regulate the Police" was passed in May 1846, ushering in the start of a modern police force. The next year saw the founding of the New York Academy of Medicine, which was dedicated to raising the standards of medical practice and promoting public health. The city's water supply no longer had to depend on wells but instead used the abundant clean water piped into Manhattan via the iron pipes of the Croton Aqueduct, which opened in 1842. In the early 1850s, granite paving stones replaced round cobblestones on the streets and legislation for Central Park was finally approved.

Thus, New York had begun to assume the characteristics of a great city. Those who saw the aqueduct

New York in 1849, looking north from Trinity Church on Wall Street. A wood engraving by S. Weekes after E. Purcell. *(I. N. Phelps Stokes Collection, Miriam and Ira D. Wallach Division of Arts, Prints and Photographs, The New York Public Library [Astor, Lenox, and Tilden Foundations])*

and the park merely as tax burdens resisted them, but forward thinkers such as William Cullen Bryant, editor of the *Evening Post*, promoted them. Although settlements such as Yorkville and Manhattanville, which were actually rural villages, were established on the north end of the island, the heavily populated area of the city ended at 23rd Street. Only four of the free schools in the city were north of this line.[2] Unlike Boston, its rival for eminence among the cities, New York had no comprehensive system of public education. In 1805, free, nonsectarian schools opened in Manhattan when a number of concerned citizens formed the Free (later Public) School Society, which was awarded a share of the New York State Common School Fund.

By 1838, the emergence of an organized labor movement in New York City, struggles among political factions, and sectarian controversies over school funding created momentum for universal education. To resolve the sectarian controversies over control of the New York State Common School Fund, the city established a Board of Education in 1842. Representatives from each ward, the smallest political unit in the city, sat on the new board and set up free, nonsectarian schools, which were financed by the Common School Fund and local taxation. The schools in each ward were governed by both the central board and elected ward trustees. By 1846, each of the eighteen wards in the city had a primary school offering the first three years of education and a grammar school responsible for another four. The Public School Society also operated a school in each ward, but as the number of ward schools increased, the need for these additional schools diminished. Thus, the Board of Education took control of the Public School Society schools in 1853.

The curriculum of these early schools included instruction in reading and writing, music, drawing, and physical training, with science, history, and civics added in the higher grades. Instruction was advertised, although seldom given, in algebra and the "grammar of astronomy, chemistry and the other sciences."[3] Prior to 1847, graduates of these schools, who were fourteen or fifteen years of age, could not continue their education unless they could afford to attend private academies or colleges. Although New York had several active cultural institutions, it lacked an institution of higher learning commensurate with the size and ambition of the city. Columbia College (founded in 1754) and the newer University of the City of New York (founded in 1831), now known as New York University, had a total combined enrollment of 245 students. Columbia, far from being the large, dynamic institution it later became, was "aristocratic in social attitude and resolutely classical in curriculum," with strong ties to the Episcopal Church.[4] The University of the City of New York was nondenominational but struggling financially and educationally. The city was ready for publicly financed higher education.

The role of Townsend Harris is essential to this story. A successful merchant in the chinaware business, Harris came from a large family from Sandy Hill (now Hudson), New York. Although his formal education was cut short by poverty, his family loved reading and valued education. He settled in New York City and joined an older brother in business, becoming active both in the Democratic politics of the ninth ward and with the volunteer firefighters. In the world of New York politics of the 1840s, Harris enjoyed a reputation for patience, persuasion, and conviviality. He represented the ninth ward in 1841–42 as commissioner of the School Fund and then as one of the two commissioners for the ward on the Board of Education from 1842 to 1844. He ran successfully for this post again in 1846 and was elected president of the Board of Education.

Following his election, Harris promptly proposed expanding publicly funded educational opportunities

In the fields of public education and diplomacy, Townsend Harris (1804–78) must rank as one of the most creative and forward-looking Americans of the nineteenth century. Born in upstate New York, he had little formal schooling, but his family loved reading and valued education, and he remained something of a student all his life. Harris taught himself to read French, Spanish, and Italian and favored the teaching of these languages in the schools. For more than twenty years, he was associated with his brothers in the chinaware trade in lower Manhattan. In 1846, Harris was elected to the presidency of the New York City Board of Education, giving him the opportunity to advance his belief that the city should provide publicly supported higher education. As legislation for the Free Academy was being drafted and then debated in Albany in March and April of 1847, Harris responded to those who opposed the idea—mostly the Whig Party press and its correspondents—with facts and closely reasoned arguments. He envisioned a Free Academy that would not only prepare young men to enter the professions, but would enrich those who planned to follow careers in commerce and the practical arts. Thus, the academy's original course of study included civil engineering, bookkeeping, shorthand, and drawing. Although the first three were dropped several years later, they ultimately found an important place in the curriculum when the City College School of Engineering and School of Business and Civic Administration were established after World War I.

Harris left New York City for California in 1848 and operated a trading ship in the Far East for several years. In 1855, President Franklin Pierce chose him to be the first U.S. consul in Japan. He was assigned to negotiate the treaty of trade and friendship, a treaty to which the Japanese had agreed reluctantly following Commodore Perry's missions of 1853 and 1854. Despite his loneliness and frustration during this period, Harris succeeded in negotiating the Treaty of Edo (Tokyo) in 1858, which benefited both Japan and the United States and became the model for the treaties Japan signed soon afterwards with other western powers. He remains a hero in Japan, where his six years there have inspired legends, plays, and operas. *(City College Archives)*

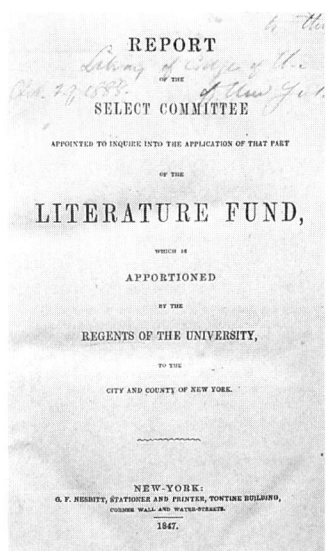

Townsend Harris wrote the committee's majority report, which proposed the establishment of the Free Academy. *(City College Archives)*

beyond the Common School. This action suggests that the subject had been important to him for some time.[5] At the board meeting of July 27, 1846, he proposed that a committee of three be appointed to look into the administration of the State Literature Fund and "the propriety of applying to the Legislature for such an alteration of the law as will permit the monies referred to be applied to the support of a high school or college for the benefit of pupils who have been educated in the public schools of the city and county."[6]

The State Literature Fund was designed to support academies and other private secondary schools. Harris maintained that the purpose of the fund, as conceived by its founders, was to extend the advantages of advanced education to all young men who could benefit from it but could not afford the cost. (Tuition at New York University was $80 a year at a time when a common laborer might earn $1 a day and a skilled one barely $5.) As it was then administered, the fund did no such thing. Most of the $5,000 spent in New York went to the Rutgers Female Institution, a proprietary school that issued stock; the Grammar School of Columbia College, then a denominational school under the governance of the Episcopal Church; and the Institution for the Deaf and Dumb.

In the report that Townsend Harris issued with Joseph S. Bosworth on January 20, 1847, he recounted the recent history of the appropriations from the fund and also listed the subjects that were not taught in the public schools: "Electricity, Civil Engineering, Analytic Geometry, Descriptive Geometry, Hydrostatics, Leveling, Mechanics, Navigation, Nautical Astronomy, Optics, Surveying, Agricultural Chemistry, Geology, Mineralogy, Natural History, Constitutional and Governmental Law, Political Economy, and the Principles of Teaching." The report, approved by the board, proposed that the legislature should turn over the city's share of the fund and supplement this amount by taxes for the purpose of "fitting up a college or academy."[7] In the struggle to get the legislation passed in Albany, some opponents maintained that the truly "deserving" could get charity scholarships to Columbia and the University of the City of New York. Using the nom de guerre "Plain Truth," Harris responded in a letter to the *Courier and Enquirer* that many of these so-called scholarships were really offers of "free" attendance in return for a donation. In addition, Harris regarded the idea of "charity schools" and "charity scholarships" as contrary to a democracy; he believed that young men of all backgrounds should mix freely at his proposed college. "Open the doors to all—let the children of the rich and the poor take their seats together, and know of no distinction save that of industry, good conduct and intellect."[8] The editor of the *Courier*, Colonel James Watson Webb, a wealthy and outspoken New Yorker, opposed the idea of a free academy. While Webb was writing editorials against the academy, his son Alexander was preparing for admission to West Point. Ironically, West Point gradu-

The Free Academy Building, located on the southeast corner of 23rd Street and Lexington Avenue, was designed by James Renwick, Jr., then a promising young architect about to be awarded the commission for St. Patrick's Cathedral in New York City. The academy building was small, with its 23rd Street facade only 125 feet in length. As prototypes, Renwick used Belgian and Dutch town halls. The basic form and fenestration of the building were derived from the King's College Chapel at Cambridge, England. The building was constructed of red brick, which was originally covered with a reddish-brown stucco finish that simulated stone and contrasted with the red sandstone trim and finials. The original plan divided the interior space into eighteen classrooms and a chapel or assembly hall. Gaslights, a warm-air heating system, and drinking fountains made the building very modern for 1848. Real slate blackboards and cherry-wood desks (with stools that had backs!) impressed the first students as the height of luxury. The total cost for the building and its furnishings came to just $68,000—$2,000 less than the city had allocated. This photograph was taken around 1900. *(City College Archives)*

ate General Alexander Stewart Webb later became president of the College of the City of New York (Free Academy) and devoted thirty-three years of his life to its advancement. Once the academy was established, however, the elder Webb softened his position and exerted his influence to make the school an important institution of higher learning.

Bills to establish the Free Academy were introduced into the New York State Legislature in February 1847. They eventually passed both houses and were signed by the sympathetic Whig governor John Young on May 7, 1847. Although the portion of the Literature Fund earmarked for New York City was to help finance the new venture, the legislators understood that support from local taxation was also needed. The Free Academy Act required New York City to put the issue on the ballot as a referendum at the judicial and school board election scheduled for June 7.[9] Another month of newspaper debate followed. However, the majority of voters, encouraged by placards posted around the city urging support of a "Free Academy for the Poor Man's Children," approved the referendum by a margin of six to one (19,305 to 3,409).

Having accomplished his mission, Townsend Harris immediately turned to selecting a site for the Free Academy. He chose the northernmost edge of the city's developed area—the southeast corner of Lexington Avenue and 23rd Street. The city's acquisition of this site proved troublesome, however. In 1807, the city had reserved the 240 acres between 23rd and 34th Streets and Third to Seventh Avenues for an arsenal, a barracks, and a potter's field known as the Parade. This area was reduced in size over the decades, and in May 1847 the newly designated Madison Square Park opened on the remaining parcel of about seven acres between 23rd and 26th Streets and Broadway and Fifth Avenue. The property holders and residents of that neighborhood objected to having the Free Academy in their vicinity, maintaining that it would lower the value of their property and destroy the square itself, to which they had contributed $70,000 in private funds. Despite this objection, the Board of Education purchased the 122- by 200-foot site from the father of the artist John LaFarge. In the fall, the Common Council approved the initial funds for the erection of the building and hired James Renwick, Jr. as architect.

Only nineteen months elapsed between the successful referendum of June 1847 and the admission of the first class of 149 students in January 1849. At an opening assembly for the students and invited guests, held in the beautiful new chapel, President Horace Webster spoke words that engage us today: "The experiment is to be tried, whether the children of the people—the children of the whole people—can be educated: and whether an institution of learning of the highest grade can be successfully controlled by the popular will, not by the privileged few but by the privileged many. . . ."[10]

At the school's founding, the sponsors chose the term "academy" to ensure that the new institution would be eligible to receive money from the State Literature Fund. Private academies taught subjects from both the English curriculum (spelling, grammar and composition, arithmetic, and some geography and history) and the Latin curriculum (based on a four- or five-year curriculum in Latin and Greek with additional studies in history and mathematics). The Free Academy was unique in that it did not charge tuition while offering a curriculum that was not only strong in practical subjects but also provided an opportunity to study classical languages and literature. This curriculum was designed to fulfill the promise of an institution that sought to benefit students of various economic classes and interests. (The initial legislation required all students to enter from the "common schools" of the city; thus, in the early years some fam-

The multifunctional "chapel" of the Free Academy Building, with its Gothic windows and arched colonnades, served as an assembly hall and seated up to 1,300. Here the entire student body and the faculty gathered daily to hear the president read from the Old Testament, make announcements, and, eight weeks into each term, dismiss those students who were not maintaining satisfactory grades. Howard Greene, an alumnus of the class of 1902, recalled: "The memories of the chapel are perhaps more numerous than those associated with any other part of the building. It was the scene of 'oratory' and remarks, class elections, class plays, the Alumni reception, and a host of minor events. . . ." (Mosenthal and Horne, *The City College*, p. 346). In this photograph, the class of 1905, the next-to-last class to spend its entire career in the old building, is assembled in front of a decoration inspired by the Civil War. On June 21, 1907, more than 1,000 graduates of the college crowded into the chapel for the last time. Representatives of each class from 1853 to 1907 sang their class songs and listened to John Hardy, valedictorian of the first class, deliver a valedictory speech to the old building. Then the class members filed out, the lights were extinguished, and the seventy-three-year-old Hardy locked the chapel door. *(City College Archives)*

ilies removed their boys from tutors and private academies and enrolled them in the public schools so that they could gain admittance.)

By the end of the century, the curriculum had slowly evolved into five courses of study: Classical, Latin-French, Modern Language, Scientific, and Mechanical. The Mechanical course of study, under the leadership of Professor Alfred G. Compton, a member of the first class of 1853, formed the basis for the future School of Engineering. The rigorous mathematics curriculum became a hallmark of the school. An excellent faculty helped establish the reputation of the mathematics department as well as the other academic divisions.

Although graduation was the ideal, attendance for a few years, or even one year, was considered advantageous at a time when professional schools did not regularly require a bachelor's degree for admission and many jobs could be filled by those able to read, write,

Horace Webster (1794–1871), president of the Free Academy from 1849 to 1869, was a Vermonter, a "Green Mountain Man" who grew up among people to whom the Revolutionary War was a vivid memory. Toward the close of the War of 1812, he received an appointment as a cadet at West Point and graduated in 1818 at the head of his class. He taught mathematics at the Point until 1826 and then became the first professor of mathematics and intellectual philosophy at Hobart (then Geneva) College in upstate New York.

Webster reflected the conservative standards of his era. He came to the Free Academy with decided ideas about the centrality of mathematics in a college curriculum and about discipline. The lack of a high school system in New York City during most of the nineteenth century brought students who were as young as fourteen to the Free Academy. Maintaining order in the face of this abundant male adolescent energy occupied much of Webster's attention. He imported West Point discipline, based on a demerit system, believing that severity of manner in a teacher created respect in the student and enabled him to learn. The number of demerits a student received could affect his academic standing. Webster also instructed the senior class in moral philosophy. He had a humane side, however, and the students affectionately referred to him as "Pop." *(City College Archives)*

Admissions procedures at City College varied during the nineteenth century. The early students, who were recommended by their grammar school principals, were required to pass a "good examination," administered orally, in spelling, reading, writing, English grammar, geography, arithmetic, and the history of the United States. Within two decades, written examinations were also required; however, the oral tradition was eventually discontinued when the number of candidates increased. Reflecting the improvements in public schools, knowledge of algebra up to simple equations became a requirement later in the century. By the early 1880s, the passing grade on the entrance examination was raised to 75 percent because the facilities had become so overcrowded. A review of the examination of 1892 revealed that 50 percent of the applicants were "deficient" in their knowledge of English grammar and 30 percent were deficient in mathematics. Henry Kates Krowl, a graduate of 1898 and future professor of English at the college, wrote: "The boys soon formed the opinion that the . . . instructors had these merits: they assigned long lessons, especially before each holiday; they gave low marks to stimulate efforts, and they told us at least once each hour that we had been badly prepared in the public schools."

Admissions registers of the nineteenth century consistently list the occupations of the students' fathers, but list those of mothers only in the case of widows—and these women are frequently described as lodging housekeepers, a designation that tells its own story. The occupations of parents reflect the cross-section of backgrounds that Townsend Harris hoped to see at the college. They also indicate much about the kinds of trades and professions prevalent in New York in the mid-nineteenth century. Butcher, gas fitter, ship-joiner, carpenter, laborer, blacksmith, clergyman, flour merchant, tobacconist, and porter were some of the occupations listed.

Nineteenth-century students received grades for the year based on daily "recitations" in class and on the results of written examinations held in February and June or July.

All during the nineteenth century, the best "senior orations," as judged by the faculty, were read at commencement. Each student prepared an essay, which was revised and then carefully copied and frequently enhanced with pen flourishes and illustrations. The 1863 commencement was scheduled to take place on July 14, but the Draft Riots of July 13–16 delayed it. Hartt's oration was evidently composed too soon to reflect the Union victory at the Battle of Gettysburg (July 1–3), as he comments that the Confederate armies owed their successes at Chancellorsville and elsewhere to a unity of purpose that the Union armies lacked. Hartt died the year after the war ended. *(City College Archives)*

and do common arithmetic. Consequently, large entering classes and small graduating classes were typical of the college during the nineteenth century. The expectations were high and rigid. The first or "preparatory" year was intended to ready the students for college work, but the lack of a high school system meant that they were often unprepared for the rigorous mathematics and foreign language curriculum. Not all students left for academic reasons. In 1851 the faculty conducted a survey of the reasons why students left the Academy. The reasons cited, in addition to academic deficiency, included entering business, illness, transfer to another college, and "going to a plantation."

In the late 1860s Charles A. Dana began to attack the college in editorials printed in his *New York Sun*. He claimed that too few students graduated from the college and that it mainly benefited the rich. The chairman of the Board of Trustees noted: "The majority of the students of our college are from families depending for their support upon their own industry. They come to school just as long as they can be spared from productive pursuits . . . It is to be lamented that so few find it convenient to complete the course, but it is a great thing for the young men and a great thing for the city, that such a multitude can spend two or more years upon the higher studies. . . ."[11] Renewing the debate of 1847, Lucius Robinson, a Democratic governor, stated in the *New York Herald* that a "sufficient common school education" was enough for good citizenship in a democracy, and that further education made the children of poor, working, and artisan classes discontented and sapped their initiative.[12] President Webb and the alumni made eloquent appeals for the college, citing the struggles many students had to undergo to stay in school and the numerous successes of its alumni. Petitions to promote popular support circulated widely in the city. Webb proved that the college was being run

Although the early graduating classes were small, commencement audiences were too large to be housed in the chapel. Initially, the Free Academy used the assembly rooms of Niblo's Gardens at Broadway and Prince Street, but the Academy of Music on the northeast corner of 14th Street and Irving Place became the preferred venue after 1854. At the commencements, graduates, parents, and illustrious guests sat under the gaslights in the white and gold hall to see awards bestowed, hear orations from leading members of the graduating class, and listen to musical selections. Starting in the 1870s, "Class Days" activities occupied the afternoon, as students conducted a humorous ceremony of their own. After the evening graduation, the new alumni held a midnight ceremony, "the planting of the ivy," proceeded by a torchlight procession. When the 4,000-seat Academy of Music closed in 1886, commencements were moved to Carnegie Hall (designed by William Tuthill, class of 1875). Finally, in June 1908, the college was able to hold commencements in its own buildings, with the first one taking place in the Great Hall of the main building on St. Nicholas Heights. By the late 1920s, the number of parents and guests outgrew the Great Hall, so the ceremony was transferred to the college's Lewisohn Stadium. *(City College Archives)*

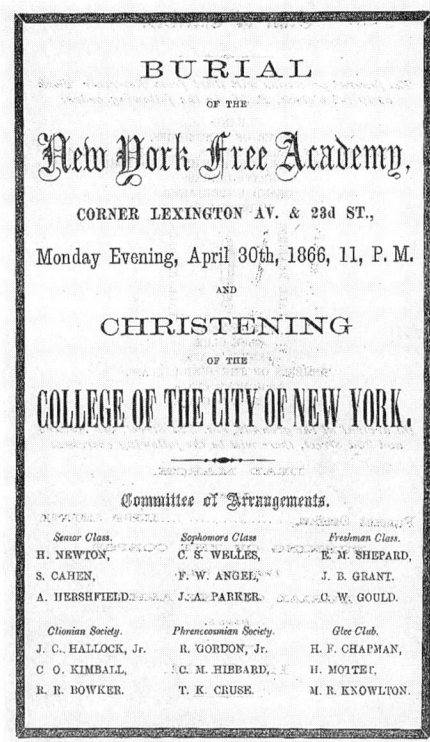

As Free Academy alumni grew in number and some began careers outside of New York, they found that the name "academy" caused confusion as to the level of work they had completed, even though the legislature had authorized the academy to confer baccalaureate degrees. After a five-year effort, both houses of the legislature passed a bill effecting a name change, which was signed by the governor. Students welcomed the new official collegiate title by adopting college colors (lavender and black) and celebrated with a torchlight procession and ceremony, which began on the night of April 30, 1866, and lasted into the early morning of May 1. After assembling at the Croton Reservoir—now the site of the New York Public Library—they marched in procession to East 23rd Street, carrying a coffin of textbooks, which they buried in the front yard of the building. Robert Abbe, later a distinguished physician and researcher but in 1866 a humble sub-freshman, wrote forty years later: "Let us recall the forming of classes in procession—each man with his torch—marching and counter-marching, shouting and echoing, crowding and jostling, within and without that old iron railing [in front of the academy building]; thronging the streets, bullying policemen, anathematizing Columbians. We owned the town that night" (Mosenthal and Horne, *The City College*, 240).

President Webster was not enthusiastic about the new name. An alumnus who told him that the name "college" conferred a higher educational status than that of "academy" received the proud retort: "Is there any higher educational institution anywhere in the world than the West Point Military ACADEMY?" (*College Mercury*, 24 [May 1903]:167). *(City College Archives)*

economically and that its faculty taught more hours than their colleagues at the University of the City of New York and at Columbia. These efforts proved successful, leading to the defeat of a bill that had been introduced in the legislature to repeal the legislation establishing City College.

The academy grew in both reputation and size in the decades following its controversial beginnings. It was renamed the College of the City of New York in 1866, and after the ceremonial "burial" of the old academy, it took its rightful place with similar institutions in New York City. Graduates of the college became recognized leaders in a variety of professions, and the prestige of a degree from the College of the City of New York (known informally as City College) increased. More students vied for places in its freshman classes, and the original building, meant to house 400, became too small.

By the 1890s space became a critical issue. Despite the construction of an annex and a laboratory, several hundred students still crowded into the original building with its limited capacity. Many sites were proposed for a new campus, but funds were not obtained until 1895, when the state legislature authorized an initial expenditure of up to $600,000 to purchase property. After considering forty locations, the Board of Trustees chose the two-block parcel between St. Nicholas Terrace and Convent Avenue from 138th to 140th Streets. Ultimately, another parcel of land was added that extended west to Amsterdam Avenue. In 1897, the board held a design competition and from the eight submissions selected the collegiate, or "Tudor," Gothic design of George B. Post.

Post, best known as the architect of the New York Stock Exchange, modified his original designs to accommodate changes in the mission of the college. The result was an integrated campus of five buildings, which included the main classroom and administrative

Civil War heroes made popular college presidents, and City College's hero was Alexander Stewart Webb (1835–1911), president of the college from 1869 to 1902. Like Webster, Webb was a West Point graduate, class of 1855. He taught mathematics at the Point but soon saw active service in the Civil War, serving first as an artillery officer and then as a brigade commander. Webb's Civil War reputation was made during the Battle of Gettysburg, where, as brigade general of volunteers, he and his men occupied the Bloody Angle and withstood Pickett's charge on July 3, 1863. Wounded himself, he saw half of his men killed. General George Meade, his commanding officer, wrote that his bravery was "not surpassed by any general on the field" (Charles F. Lydecker, "The Second President," in Mosenthal and Horne, *The City College*, 118). Webb's reputation as a successful and strong leader, an authentic hero, and a man of unshakable integrity was an important factor in his success as president of the college. Conservative in his educational views, he opposed the development of the elective system at the undergraduate level, maintaining to the end his belief in a rigid curriculum in the arts and sciences, which stressed mathematics and languages. (*City College Archives*)

Alfred Compton (1835–1913) liked to recall that he had been "born within the sound of Bow Bells," a reference to his Cockney origin. This Londoner was seven years old when he was brought to New York, where his father established a piano factory "on the wooded heights of Bellevue fronting the East River" in the neighborhood of 25th Street. A member of the first class at the Free Academy, he was appointed to a tutorship upon his graduation in 1853. In 1869, the chair of applied mathematics became vacant, and Compton filled it for forty years, teaching not only mathematics but also astronomy and physics. He developed a three-year postgraduate course in civil engineering, which he taught for eighteen years in addition to performing his appointed duties. Compton also wrote textbooks on woodworking, metalworking, and the speed lathe for the after-hours workshop course approved by the faculty in 1883. By 1890, City College, under Compton's direction, offered a five-year mechanical course that included a full component of liberal arts and sciences along with workshop courses. Compton's leadership provided the foundation for the future City College School of Engineering.

As a teacher, Compton was demanding but fair, and his systematic presentations and clear explanations smoothed the way for students who found mathematics, physics, and astronomy difficult. Compton also trained the younger instructors in his methods and in the art of good blackboard demonstrations.

During his student years, Compton formed a lifelong friendship with his classmate James Rich Steers. Both were enthusiastic hikers who over a period of fifty years covered thousands of miles in the Adirondacks. They were also keen botanists, and Compton was so skilled at camp craft, in addition to his extensive knowledge of applied science, that his friend Lewis Sayre Burchard wrote: "If Compton were washed up like Robinson Crusoe on some great new island with the necessary natural resources and given a few tools from the ship, and say a century of life and unskilled labor without limit, but without a book, he could reproduce civilization. . . ." (Lewis Sayre Burchard, "A Chat About Professor Compton by an Old Graduate," *City College Quarterly* 10 [March 1914]:13). *(City College Archives)*

The Physics and Chemistry Laboratory represented one of Alexander Stewart Webb's successes in obtaining badly needed expansion funds from New York City. It was constructed in 1883, just east of the academy building on 23rd Street. The laboratory had three large skylights, a "chemical room," a "physical laboratory," and workshops. The laboratories allowed the students to put into practice what they had heard and seen at the lectures and demonstration experiments of Professor Robert Ogden Doremus, professor of chemistry and physics from 1863 to 1903. Doremus's lectures were popular with all students, and he was one of the few members of the nineteenth-century faculty to have a national reputation. He had assisted Professor John Draper of the University of the City of New York (NYU) in taking the earliest photographs of the human face, and he experimented with "Tithonic Rays," which foreshadowed the discovery of the X-ray. Doremus's civic-mindedness led him to participate in the founding of the New York City Board of Health and the New York Medical College. With his wide travel experience and prominent place in society, he seemed the incarnation of a sophisticated man of the world to many students of the college. *(City College Archives)*

William Hallett Greene (B.S., 1884) is the first graduate of City College who can be identified as an African American. His father was a coachman, and the family lived at 127 West 31st Street, a region of the West Side that, along with the Greenwich Village neighborhood, was then home to many of Manhattan's African Americans. Described in the *College Mercury* as "very popular," Greene was a member of the cabinet or inner circle of Phrenocosmia, one of the college's two literary and debating societies, and was elected recording secretary of the senior class of 1884. He served on the photography committee of his class, negotiating with photography studios to find the best prices for the cabinet and carte-de-visite photographs that seniors were required to obtain. Greene was one of the 20 young men who graduated in 1884—survivors of an entering class of 250. After receiving his degree, Greene joined the United States Signal Corps, then the branch of the army responsible for military communications, meteorological studies, and related work. *(City College Archives)*

building, the preparatory high school, a gymnasium, the "chemical building," and a building for the mechanical course. This last building was later extended through an addition onto Amsterdam Avenue.

The groundbreaking ceremony took place early in 1903. Classes began on the St. Nicholas Heights campus in September 1907, and an elaborate dedication ceremony was held in May 1908, at which an exuberant President John Huston Finley played host to Mark Twain and dignitaries from the city, state, and nation. The IRT subway station at 137th Street opened in the fall of 1904, and the rapid expansion of the transit system provided access to the college from all boroughs of New York. President Finley reaped the benefits of the long struggle for a new home and acceded to the demands of the faculty who had lobbied for a less rigid curriculum.

By 1906, the college had graduated 2,911 men, 2,000 of whom still resided in New York City. Based on a count of those who attended for a year or more, Richard Bowker, an early graduate, estimated that

> Probably a thirtieth of the entire male population of the city above the age of fifteen, have been students in the college. Nearly every family in New York, except among the latest immigrants, has had directly or indirectly some knowledge of the advantages of the college. . . . Many of its students come from the poorest classes, the fathers working harder that their boys may have a "better chance" than themselves, and of these many are the children of foreign parents who speak little if any English, for whom the public schools and the college are the living link between the bright future which they seek for their children and the dark past from which they escaped.[13]

In a speech given at the dedication ceremonies of the uptown campus, President Finley defined his position eloquently: "If the poorest and richest are alike to be given their share of the heritage of men, the college

Although John Huston Finley grew up on his family's farm in Illinois, he was associated with New York City for most of his career. After graduating from Knox College in Galesburg, Illinois, he studied political science at The Johns Hopkins University and then returned to Knox in the 1890s as its president. Finley moved to Princeton as professor of politics in 1900 on the recommendation of Woodrow Wilson, his Hopkins classmate and the future Princeton president. His growing prestige brought him to the attention of the Board of Trustees of City College as a man well suited to move the college into the twentieth century.

As the college's third president, Finley brought a fresh approach to the students, ending the old demerit system and supporting athletics and student government. "Read a book, take a walk, make a friend," he advised the students. His winning personality and boundless energy were totally dedicated to gaining increased civic support for the college. As president, he demonstrated the ability to select good administrators and inspire them with his own enthusiasm. At his inauguration on September 20, 1903, on the stage of Carnegie Hall, Finley accepted the seal of the college and then said: "I believe in a higher education for the people, supported by the people, and having in its purpose the good of all the people" (College of the City of New York. *Programme of the Installation of John H. Finley*, 1903).

During his presidency, Finley made brilliant use of the college's new campus, especially its Great Hall, as a forum for national and international visitors. Finley left the college in 1913 to become the commissioner of education for New York State, but in 1921 he began a new career as associate editor of *The New York Times*. Until shortly before his death in 1940, he remained active at the *Times*, retiring as editor in 1938. *(City College Archives)*

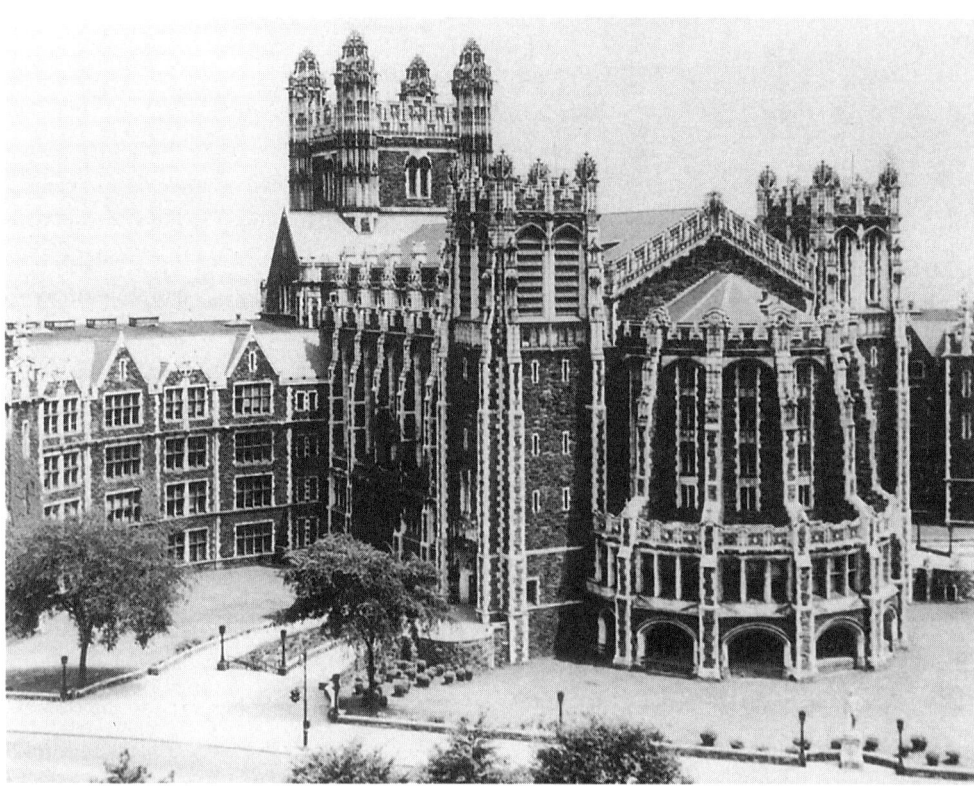

Shepard Hall is the signature building of the St. Nicholas Heights campus, which City College occupied in September 1907. The original five-building design of George Browne Post used Manhattan schist with contrasting white terra cotta trim for buildings described as "collegiate Gothic" and "Tudor Gothic." Shepard—originally known simply as Main Building—stands on the east side of Convent Avenue, directly overlooking St. Nicholas Park. Post made this building the center of interest of the Gothic Quadrangle. Finialed buttresses, towers of varying heights, and rich detail helped give the building its pivotal role in the scheme. The wings initially housed classrooms and offices in the humanities, social sciences, physics, and biology, with the president's office at the end of the central corridor. The Great Hall, which forms an apse in the center of the building and rises to 169 feet at its highest point, became the site of commencements, public organ concerts, and programs and lectures from prominent national and international figures. *(City College Archives)*

must come in the midst of men and their homes. It must, moreover, carry its horizons with it and not let the tall buildings shut it in. . . . I give myself as hostage for these eager, noisy, ambitious boys and young men, that they will bring back to the City even more than they have received."[14] John Finley concluded his presidency of the College of the City of New York in 1913, and Sidney E. Mezes from the University of Texas succeeded him.

When President Finley's tenure ended, the college had a new physical plant that was not yet overcrowded, a curriculum that allowed electives, and the elements of a rich student life. John Huston Finley envisioned that the College of the City of New York would develop into a great university of the city. As an editor of *The New York Times* in the 1920s and 1930s, he would bring the details of that development to the public.

Notes

1. Valentine, *Manual of the Corporation of the City of New York*, 286–88.
2. Ibid., 237–45.
3. *Journal of Commerce*, (5 June 1847), as cited in Cosenza, *The Establishment of the City College of the City of New York as the Free Academy in 1847*, 194.
4. Bender, *New York Intellect*, 91.
5. Mario E. Cosenza, "The Life, Letters and Papers of Townsend Harris." Unpublished typescript, n.d., Chapter III: 2–6, in Cosenza Collection, Archives and Special Collections, City College of the City University of New York. See also Cosenza, *The Establishment of the City College of the City of New York as the Free Academy in 1847*, 7–13.
6. New York City Board of Education, *Minutes of Meeting of July 29, 1846*, as published in Cosenza, *The Establishment of the City College of the City of New York as the Free Academy in 1847*, 15.

Harris High School, the college's preparatory high school, evolved out of its original "sub-freshman" or preparatory year. In the decade following the creation of a public high school system in New York City, the one-year course was expanded into an accelerated three-year high school program. Admission to Harris High was selective, and its graduates—many of whom went on to matriculate at the college—form a roster of high achievers. A few representative names are author Herman Wouk, actor Cornel Wilde, politician Adam Clayton Powell, lyricist Ira Gershwin, scientist Jonas Salk, news commentator David Schonbrun, and playwright Sidney Kingsley. In 1930, overcrowding on the St. Nicholas Heights campus resulted in the transfer of the school to the top floors of the City College School of Business building on East 23rd Street. It flourished there until 1942, when the development of specialized high schools created pressures that ultimately led to Mayor LaGuardia's decision to "defund" the school to force its closure. A revived Townsend Harris Alumni Association succeeded in having the Board of Education create a new coeducational high school on the Queens College campus, which carries on the Townsend Harris name and its tradition of scholarship.

---

7. *Report of the Select Committee Appointed to Inquire into the Application of That Part of the Literature Fund Which Is Apportioned by the Regents of the University of the City and County of New York*. The third member of the committee, James J. King, a man of substantial wealth and position, issued a minority report (*Report of Mr. King from the Committee Appointed to Inquire into the Application of the Literature Fund . . .*).

8. Townsend Harris to editors of the *Courier and Enquirer* (15 March 1847) as printed in Cosenza, *The Establishment of the City College of the City of New York as the Free Academy in 1847*, 81.
9. For the legislative history of the Free Academy, see *Journal of the New York State Senate*, 1847, 70th Session, 436, 446, 461–62, 508, 514, 536, 566; *Journal of the New York State Assembly*, 1847, Vols. I and II, 1084, 1217, 1221, 1238–40, 1262; *Laws of the State of New York*, first meeting, 70th Session, 1847, 208–212; and Chapter 206 of the *Laws of New York State* for 1847. The bill entitled "An Act Authorizing the Board of Education of the City and County of New York to Establish a Free Academy in Said City" passed May 7, 1847 [pursuant to Section 14, Article 7, of the Constitution] and signed by the Governor, constitutes the first charter of what became the City College of New York.
10. "Address of Horace Webster," in *Addresses Delivered upon the Occasion of the Opening of the Free Academy*, 27.
11. *Minutes of the Board of Trustees of the College of the City of New York*, 1873, 2–3.
12. *New York Herald* (January 13, 1878), 8.
13. Richard R. Bowker, "The College of the Past," in Mosenthal and Horne, *The City College*, 19–20.
14. "Address by President Finley," *City College Quarterly* 4 (1908), 94–95.

Although the St. Nicholas Heights campus contained a state-of-the-art gymnasium, no provision had been made for outdoor athletic activity. President John Finley persuaded philanthropist Adolph Lewisohn to fund a stadium on land provided by the New York City Parks Department between Convent and Amsterdam Avenues and 136th to 138th Streets. Designed by Arnold Brunner, the stadium was a large half-oval that originally had an open view to the campus and the city. The primary building material was reinforced concrete, and the major stylistic feature was a peristyle of sixty-four precast Tuscan Doric columns. The inaugural event at the stadium on May 29, 1915, almost as if to highlight its classical look, was a performance of *The Trojan Women* by Euripides, produced by the popular English playwright and director Harley Granville-Barker. The college quickly put the field to use for baseball, track, and eventually football, as well as for ROTC exercises.

Its summer concert series made Lewisohn Stadium known all over New York City and was a feature of New York City summers for fifty years. The driving force behind Stadium Concerts, Inc., which produced the concerts, was Minnie Guggenheimer, whose enthusiasm and financial backing helped thousands to hear performers from the concert hall and operatic stage for as little as twenty-five cents. "Emerging" artists gave some of their first concerts at the stadium. Marian Anderson performed in 1925, and George Gershwin played his "Rhapsody in Blue" and conducted "An American in Paris" on August 26, 1929. That decade saw performers as varied as the Hall Johnson Negro Choir, the Denishawn Dancers, and Nelson Eddy on the

Establishing Public Higher Education in New York City 21

stage of Lewisohn. One of the last performers was pianist Earl Wild, who performed in an annual Gershwin memorial concert in the early 1960s. From the beginning, the performers competed with noise from the boats and barges on the Hudson and from street traffic; by the early 1960s, increasing noise from the heavier airline traffic had become a constant accompaniment. Audiences diminished, and the 10,000 seats were no longer filled on summer nights.

In 1965, City College made public its master plan, which included demolition of Lewisohn Stadium, and held its last commencement there in 1973. The North Academic Center, which opened in 1984, provided classrooms, a new library, and dining and student union facilities. The state-of-the-art Herman Goldman Center for Sports and Recreation opened on the South Campus in 1993. Adolph Lewisohn intended his gift to benefit not just City College but thousands of New Yorkers who were not affiliated with the school. For half a century, his hopes were triumphantly realized, and his name survives on the spacious Lewisohn Plaza of the North Academic Center. *(City College Archives)*

2 Women Enter onto the Scene

In early nineteenth-century America, higher education was primarily for men. The "cult of domesticity" encouraged the middle- and upper-class woman to confine her activities to the home, family, and church, and this dominant philosophy was rarely challenged. The education that women did receive during the first half of the century was adapted to the perceived limitations of their minds and bodies. Since mothers were the primary influence on the morality of the younger generation and were the preservers of hearth and home, their education served mainly to benefit society.

This cult of "true womanhood" crossed the ocean to the young republic from England, France, and Germany, and, as in Europe, advice manuals were published to aid the American woman. The most notable American writer on this theme was Catherine Beecher, daughter of the Presbyterian minister and temperance advocate Lyman Beecher and sister of Harriet Beecher Stowe. Catherine Beecher, believing that women had political importance because of their dominance in the home, was an early advocate for the education of women. In her many textbooks and treatises, she tried to instruct the American woman in her proper responsibilities. Among her works were *A Treatise on Domestic Economy* (1841) and *The Duty of American Women to Their Country* (1845).

Women's academies and seminaries were founded in the early nineteenth century, championed by Catherine Beecher and such other advocates of women's education as Mary Lyon and Emma Willard. The curricula usually emphasized the domestic arts and seldom included the subjects studied by men. Wealthy families who could afford not only the tuition but also the release of a daughter from familial responsibilities supported these newly formed institutions. This growth in female education reached its peak in the 1850s, when normal schools and public high schools became viable alternatives for women.

Change was already in the air. The Seneca Falls Convention in 1848 raised the conscience of the more daring women. The appeal for full citizenship for women, which included suffrage, made women responsible not only for the correct rearing of their children but also for their own rights as citizens. This view directly challenged the Victorian doctrine of separate spheres for men and women. Consequently, some young women saw in higher education an opportunity to maintain a role outside the family and become autonomous.

Teaching was the profession closest to the domestic scene and consequently the most acceptable for women to pursue. Women were considered qualified to teach because of temperament, moral purity, and a disposition to teach the young. Although many of the teachers in the republic were male, women entered the profession early in the nineteenth century. Often, these female teachers were only a chapter or two ahead of their pupils, a situation that had to be remedied. Normal schools, which were intended to meet the need for more qualified teachers, were established by state legislators in New York and other states. In the 1867 edition of *The Means and Ends of Universal Education*, the author reflected:

> *Normal Schools are essential* to the complete success of any system of popular education. The necessity for their establishment can not fail to be apparent to any one at all competent to judge, when he considers the early age at which young persons of both sexes generally enter upon the business of school-teaching—or, perhaps I may more appropriately say, of "keeping" school; for the majority of them can hardly be regarded as competent to teach.[1]

The normal school movement can be traced to the attempts of early advocates of female education to establish institutions of higher education for women. The Female College at Macon, Georgia; Wesleyan Female College in Cincinnati, Ohio; Oberlin College in Oberlin, Ohio; and Elmira College in Elmira, New York, were among the schools that served as trailblazers while perpetuating domestic values in the curricula. However, when Vassar College, established by Matthew Vassar in Poughkeepsie, New York, opened its doors in 1865, a new era in higher education for women began. The new philosophy challenged the previously held views of the capabilities of the daughters of the republic, and rigorous subjects in the sciences as well as the arts were introduced into the curriculum.

The establishment of normal schools was closely linked with economic and social developments in America. An economy increasingly based on commerce, industry, and technology required a work force with a higher degree of literacy than was needed earlier in the century. The influx of new immigrants that began in the 1840s swelled into a tide by the 1890s and created a need for "Americanization" programs in the schools. More and better-qualified teachers were required. Consequently, public support for advanced education in the United States gained momentum, and teacher-training colleges were established with state support. The Morrell Act of 1862 inaugurated support at the federal level by providing for grants of public lands for educational facilities (the land grant colleges). New York City became the first city to create municipally funded institutions of higher education.

The State of New York made some early efforts to train teachers. In 1826 Governor DeWitt Clinton recommended the establishment of a seminary for the education of teachers based on the prevailing belief that the academy was the proper institution for teacher training. Unfortunately, Clinton lacked the political support to implement his proposal. Consequently, the bill he signed in 1827 proposed merely to "promote the education of teachers." In 1834, the state legislated to provide for "the better education of teachers." Women benefited from this legislation when three normal schools, open to both men and women, were estab-

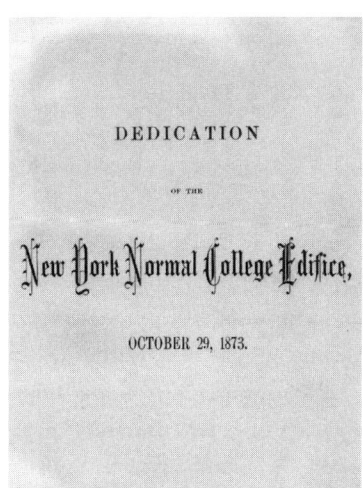

(Hunter College Archives)

lished in New York City under the aegis of the New York Public School Society, but they had all closed by 1854. In 1847, New York City set up the Free Academy for male graduates of public grammar schools. Two years later, Robert Kelly, president of the Board of Education in the city, proposed a "Free Academy" for females, but the idea was a bit ahead of the times. It was not until 1854 that the legislature authorized the founding of a similar institution for women. The momentum mounted in the late 1860s, when the Board of Education was given the responsibility of preparing teachers for the common schools. Since the Free Academy did not adequately fill this need, the establishment of a normal and high school for females was finally approved on November 17, 1869.

The first class, which was selected by competitive examination, was admitted on February 14, 1870, with 1,068 pupils marching two by two into the school's home at 694 Broadway. Mayor Abraham Oakey Hall, in a speech delivered at the dedication of the new institution on March 24, 1870, stated: "[T]he greatness of New-York was obscured by great defects, and its growing advancement in education had hitherto been impeded by the want of a normal school. For sixteen years the cry had gone up for such an institution, and at last the want was supplied." Another speaker at the event, James W. Gerard, "believed in widening the sphere of woman's labor, and giving her an opportunity to do anything for which her temperament and strength fitted her."[2]

The founding of the Normal College was a landmark in the history of the education of women in the United States. Although some grammar schools in the city offered supplementary classes, no daily high schools existed. Dr. Thomas Hunter, the first president of the Normal College, wanted the new institution to provide a constant supply of trained teachers for all city schools; thus he opened admission to both black and white students on an equal basis. The Normal College became a unique haven for women of all races, religions, and classes. President Hunter stated: "We have Jews and Gentiles and the children of almost every European nationality; dark-skinned negroes sitting beside fair-haired Scandinavians, and almost every creed under the sun is represented. . . . This is a true democratic mingling of the classes which could only exist in a Republican country like the United States."[3] The Normal College of the City of New York became the first publicly funded, tuition-free college for women in the United States, and for many years it fulfilled its original mission of preparing the majority of its graduates for teaching positions in the New York City schools. Although many graduates of City College went on to careers in the public school system, the curriculum was not specifically oriented toward pedagogy, whereas the Normal College had the utilitarian purpose of preparing women for a teaching career. Graduates of City College received a B.A. degree, but the graduates of the Normal College earned a certificate and a license to teach. It was not until after the passage of the Cantor Bill by the

---

President Thomas Hunter believed that admission, promotion, and graduation should be based on competitive examinations. Civil service reform was a contemporary issue in Congress, and President Hunter was convinced of the benefits of the democratic ideals of meritocracy. Admission was to be based on impartial standards, minimizing the power that principals and parents maintained over controlling who should be admitted to the Normal School. The examination remained, and today competitive examinations are used for admission to the elementary and high school divisions of Hunter College.

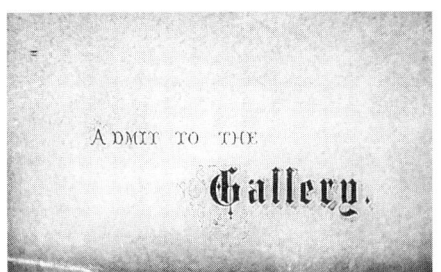

The Normal College's first commencement was held only five months after it opened. Of the ninety-seven graduates, at least two-thirds had finished the five-month supplementary course of study, qualifying them to teach in the public school. The local press extensively covered the occasion, and thousands gathered at the Academy of Music on 14th Street to witness the event. The college president's annual report in 1870 asserted: "The interest manifested in a popular free college for the education of women was absorbing, and shows that the great heart of New York always beats in harmony with true progress."
(Hunter College Archives)

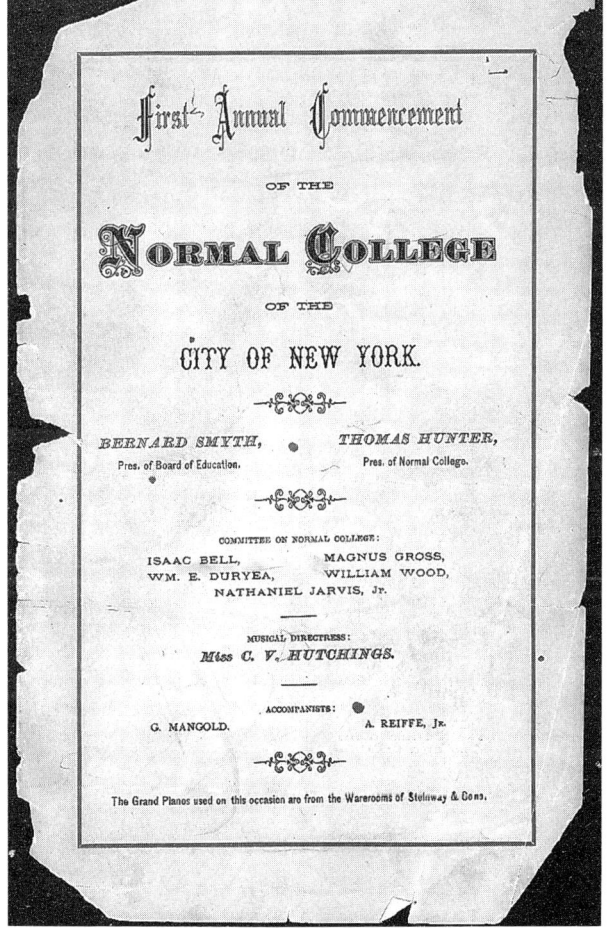

New York State Legislature in 1888 that the Normal College became a corporate body with the right to grant degrees as well as licenses.

A permanent home for the school was opened in 1873 in the semirural area of Park Avenue and 68th Street. The formal dedication took place on October 29, 1873.

> Mr. Wilson [president of the Board of Education] stepped to the reading-desk and delivered a brief address. He said that he found great pleasure in meeting so many young ladies ambitious of becoming teachers in the public schools. Their desire was a most laudable one, and full of promise for the future of this great City. Who can too highly appreciate woman's work in society? She exercises, said the speaker, an immense influence over its welfare, and shapes and directs much of its destiny. Referring to the share she has in the education of the City's masses, he said that there are ten woman teachers to-day to one of the other sex in our public schools, and they do their work admirably.[4]

The original site of the Female Normal and High School was 17 St. Mark's Place, but the school soon moved to two floors of a commercial building at 694 Broadway. In April 1870, the New York State Legislature changed the name to the Normal College of the City of New York and authorized a permanent site—Park Avenue between 68th and 69th Streets. On September 1, 1873, students entered their new building for the first time. The official dedication took place on October 29, 1873, with the mayor, the governor, the U.S. commissioner of education, and other distinguished guests in attendance. *The New York Times* of October 30, 1873, reported Mayor William Havemeyer's view that with the opening of the Free Academy, "New-York provided for the education [of] its boys; now it is equally as solicitous and provident for that of its girls. This Metropolis is like a wise mother giving all her children a fair start in the race of life." *(Hunter College Archives)*

This belief that teaching was the proper work for women prevailed during the early years of the Normal College. The usual aspiration of those in attendance was to teach only until they married, a view that was slow to change.

In fact, women did not begin to broaden their outlook and consider other options until the late 1880s, when degree-granting collegiate status was finally obtained. Professional training in law and medicine as well as graduate education also became available for qualified women at that time. In addition, a new five-year classical course was designed to raise the standards of the Normal College to conform to those of other colleges for women, such as Vassar. *The New York Times* reported in 1894: "This college is to prepare women for the many opportunities that are now open to her in the field of medicine, law, journalism, commerce and others, that are now receiving her on equal terms with men."[5]

Corresponding to the changes in the attitudes of society and the broadening of the Normal College curriculum, a variety of programs that became popular in the twentieth century had their roots in the last decades of the nineteenth century.

President Thomas Hunter suggested introducing a business course as early as the 1880s, but this proposal was not approved until 1919, when a commercial course, designed to prepare high school teachers to teach business subjects, was instituted. In addition, alumnae in the late 1880s planned and directed an extension session that the college eventually took over in the next century as evening and extension courses. Coeducation also became the subject of debate with the proposal in 1906 to merge the Normal College with the College of the City of New York. The Normal College strongly opposed the merger since such a plan would have meant loss of power and institutional integrity.[6]

Graduations from the two municipal colleges, City College and the Normal College, were major events in New York City in the nineteenth century. At the Normal College ceremony, thousands of invited guests would clamor to enter the chapel where the commencement took place. *The New York Times* reported in its June 30, 1880, edition: "At last a half door of the entrance was thrown open, and the uncomfortable throng of ladies and gentlemen was permitted to crush through slowly and scramble to the chapel." The *Times* went on: "The organ in the gallery played, and presently the graduates came filing in, in gleaming costumes, an attractive body of nearly 400 tastefully-arrayed young women, who were not less attractive to look at because it was known that they were possessed of brains as well as comeliness." *(Hunter College Archives)*

With the first wave of women college graduates in the 1880s seeking meaningful and socially acceptable career options, settlement work—the precursor of social work—became a popular alternative to teaching. Each of the "seven sister schools," as the first prestigious colleges for women in the Northeast were known, had a favorite settlement house where students gained experience while helping perform the daily functions of the institution. The alumnae of the Normal College joined this movement and in 1894 opened the Normal College Alumnae Settlement House, now known as the Lenox Hill Neighborhood Association. The association has maintained a long history of service to the community. Classes for immigrants, a day-care center for working parents, a summer camp for deserving children, and many other activities continue to be provided for the community. *(Lenox Hill Neighborhood Association Collection/Hunter College Archives)*

The early years of the Normal College produced many distinguished graduates. One such woman was Helen Gray Cone, class of 1876, who had an impressive career as a published poet, writer, and teacher. She was named Chair of the English Department at the Normal College in 1889 and was remembered for her lasting interest and participation in the extracurricular activities of her students. Her love of her alma mater can be seen in the lyrics that she wrote to the Normal College commencement song:

O good ship Alma Mater, a long farewell at last,
We're hopeful for the future, we're grateful for the past,
Sail on through sunny waters; with more than lips can tell
Of sorrow at our parting, we speak the last farewell.

(Hunter College Archives)

As the nineteenth century drew to a close, the demand for admission increased, and space in the building on 68th Street became limited. In 1907, additional rooms were rented for an annex on 93rd Street. Shortly thereafter, the old school was torn down and a new building was planned to replace it on Lexington Avenue, adjacent to the original site. The Board of Trustees of the City College granted the Normal College temporary use of the 22nd Street annex of the College of the City of New York, but the Trustees of the Normal College assumed the cost of adapting the facilities for women students. On May 4, 1908, George Samler Davis became the second president of the Normal College. President Davis was instrumental in convincing the Interborough Rapid Transit Company to build one of the stations of its new Lexington Avenue Line at 68th Street, thus linking the college with more distant areas of the city. In 1912 the first section of the new facility was completed.

The subjects that were originally taught in the New York public schools became the basis for the initial teacher training program at the Normal College. President Hunter wanted his students to gain a broad intellectual foundation in preparation for teaching. He insisted on including in the curriculum sciences, mathematics, and language to augment the pedagogy program and the more traditional home economics courses. In his annual report of 1890, President Hunter stated: "The assertion has been made that women cannot as a rule master the higher mathematics. That this is a grievous mistake has been amply proved in Professor [Joseph] Gillet's department in which young girls, of the average of eighteen, have been wrestling for the past year with the abstractions of analytical geometry and other subjects supposed by some to be beyond the comprehension of women."
(Hunter College Archives)

Literary societies for women in the 1870s and 1880s imitated the male tradition of using Greek letter names. They became important vehicles for intellectual activities beyond the classroom. Although President Hunter did not support extracurricular activities for his young women, he did consent to the formation of the Philomathean and Alpha Beta Gamma literary societies. The women in the back row are identified as Grace Merrill, Macella Kramer, Ella Sully, Jeanette Seligmann, and Sophie Mueller. In the front row are Roselle Hellenberg, Joc Munson, Luia Rotto, and Alice Mae Mahau. In 1889, the two literary societies joined to publish the *Echo,* a new student magazine. The pages of the *Echo* tell the story of student life after 1889, describing trips, summer vacations, festivals, and reunions. During this period, school galas promoted a new school spirit, as restrictions on talking and after-school activities were eased. *(Hunter College Archives)*

The new president also wanted to win full recognition of a Normal College degree by the state of New York, and he accomplished this task by December 1908. Finally, women were offered privileges equal to those of men in their educational institutions. The tightly disciplined and closely supervised student body gained a new independence, soon to be seen in an array of extracurricular activities under student control.

Other changes were instituted as well. In the fall of 1910, courses leading to the B.A. degree were offered at night and in the late afternoon. Because of the higher academic status of the liberal arts programs at the college, the name "Normal College" was no longer accurate. A change in name was proposed as early as 1904, but it was not until 1909 that President Davis mentioned the idea in his commencement address. It then

This lithograph, published in *Harper's Bazaar*, shows the major figures in the early history of the Normal College. Thomas Hunter was its president from 1870 until his retirement in 1906. He felt that eight years of grammar school education were not enough to prepare a student to be a teacher. Thus, he was instrumental in creating a three-year program of instruction—the first two years were academic and the third was devoted to pedagogy and practice teaching. During his tenure at the Normal College, President Hunter led the school from education designed to train teachers to the creation of degree-granting programs on a par with those provided for men.

Ex-Commissioner William Wood of the Board of Education became a close friend of President Hunter. He was impressed with Hunter's success as principal of No. 35, the largest and one of the most prestigious grammar schools for boys in New York City, and was converted to his educational beliefs. As commissioner, Wood tried to provide President Hunter with what he wanted, selected a site for the Normal College, and was present for its dedication.

Marguerite Merington, an 1875 graduate, was president of the alumnae association of the Normal College

took five years for a final decision on the name change to be made. The Normal College became Hunter College on April 4, 1914—an apt tribute to President Thomas Hunter, who had devoted thirty-seven years to the education of women in New York City.

From its beginnings, Hunter College was an innovator in education for women, and in the years that followed, the college distinguished itself in many areas of study, never forsaking its original mission of preparing women as teachers for the New York City school system. A distinguished roster of graduates attests to the valuable service this free, publicly supported college for women contributed to New York.

Although the institution would undergo many changes in the future, the legacy of Thomas Hunter remains.

---

from 1888 to 1892. The alumnae association, which was established when the first class graduated, was incorporated in 1889. It was instrumental in organizing many social service activities, including the creation of a loan fund for deserving students and the establishment of what became the Lenox Hill Neighborhood Association, home of the first free public kindergarten in America. During Merington's tenure as president of the association, the alumnae arranged for lectures on subjects that they felt were important to women and educators but were beyond the scope of the traditional college coursework. In 1890, the alumnae association established accredited extension classes for higher teaching licenses, which were the precursors of the evening division. Merington was a classics teacher, a playwright, and an artist who painted a portrait of the revered Thomas Hunter.

Lydia Wadleigh was selected to be the first superintendent of the Normal College. Born in New Hampshire, she was an 1841 graduate of the Academical and Theological Institution of New Hampton, where she received a diploma with the distinction "Lady and Scholar." Her outstanding abilities were shown by her success as principal of Girls School No. 47. Indeed, the first class at the Normal College included 300 young women she had brought with her from her supplementary classes held at P.S. 47. The Board of Education had established these classes to help supply teachers for the New York City schools. The 1870 annual report of the Normal College's president stated that she "had the special charge of the manners and morals of the young ladies, and has been the chief executive officer, under the President, in enforcing the necessary discipline of the College." Lydia Wadleigh died in 1888 and was memorialized in the poetry of Helen Cone. The Wadleigh Memorial Library Alcove in the Alumnae Center and one of the first public high schools in New York City were named after her.

Jenny M. Merrill was a tutor in methods of teaching for many years before becoming the first supervisor of kindergartens in New York City, a position that she held for almost two decades. She was also active in the founding of the New York Free Kindergarten Association.

The professors of the Normal College throughout the 1870s and early 1880s were all male. The seven male department heads held the rank of professor; all other faculty members were tutors. However, several of the graduates from these early years eventually moved into the professorate, and names such as Emma Requa and Helen Cone stand out as pioneers. *(Hunter College Archives)*

The alumnae association established the Wadleigh Memorial Library Alcove in the Alumnae Center. This served as the foundation of the Alumnae Library, which eventually became the college library. The alumnae raised more than $10,000 and hired a Normal College graduate, Edith Rice, as the librarian, paying her until the college took over the library in 1896. The Municipal Civil Service Commission officially appointed her to the position in 1899.

After President Hunter retired, Joseph A. Gillet became acting president. He took an active interest in the college library and made Dr. Margaret B. Wilson, a physician and head of the Department of Physiology, honorary librarian. Correspondence between Dr. Gillet and Dr. Wilson noted the increased use of the library, and consequently library hours were extended, periodicals were bound, and a listing of recent acquisitions was posted on a bulletin board. In addition, Dr. Wilson arranged for The New York Public Library to loan books to scholars overnight. During her tenure she increased the library's collection from a few thousand to 31,000 volumes. *(Hunter College Archives)*

The Normal College can claim many illustrious graduates of the early classes. Julia Richman (1855–1912), a graduate of the two-year course of the college in 1872, became a distinguished educator and a social activist. She began her career as a teacher in the New York public schools, advancing to vice-principal in 1882 and to principal of the girls' department of P.S. 77 in 1884. In 1903, the New York City Board of Education named her district superintendent.

In addition to her teaching responsibilities, Richman was the president of the Young Ladies' Charitable Union from 1876 to 1881. From 1886 to 1890, she was the first president of the Young Women's Hebrew Association, and in 1889 she founded the Educational Alliance to aid in the Americanization of Jewish immigrants. She is memorialized in the New York City high school that bears her name. *(Hunter College Archives)*

Notes

1. Mayhew, *The Means and Ends of Universal Education*, 421.
2. "Dedication of the New Institution—Interesting Exercises and Address," *The New York Times* (March 5, 1870), 2.
3. *Annual Report of the Normal College, 1886*, 39–40, as cited by Grunfeld, "Purpose and Ambiguity," 92.
4. "The Normal College. The Dedication—Interesting Exercises," *The New York Times* (October 30, 1873), 2.
5. "Normal College Graduates," *The New York Times* (June 22, 1894), as cited in Grunfeld, "Purpose and Ambiguity," 56.
6. Grunfeld, "Purpose and Ambiguity," 133–37.

3 Opportunity Grows with the City

The population of New York City was increasing rapidly by the turn of the century, as a new wave of immigrants—now primarily from Eastern Europe—arrived and settled within its boundaries. In 1900, 3.4 million people lived in the newly consolidated greater New York, but that figure quickly grew to 5.6 million by 1920. With this population explosion came the expansion of the rapid transit lines to create greater access to the outer boroughs of Brooklyn, the Bronx, and Queens and to foster residential development. At the opening of the West Side IRT in the fall of 1904, Mayor George B. McClellan predicted that the subway would ensure New York's status as a great city.[1] His prediction proved to be correct; however, one result of this growing stature was the influx of immigrants and their need for education at all levels, from kindergarten through college. Adapting to this need proved to be an especially difficult task for the municipal colleges.

By 1905, the borough with the greatest educational need was Brooklyn. Its residents campaigned for their own municipal college, thereby reviving a movement that had begun with a State Legislative Act on March 21, 1861, giving twenty-four prominent New Yorkers the authority to act as a corporate body called "The University of Brooklyn." This body was empowered to establish colleges, although not free ones such as City College and the future Normal College. Interest in the subject declined with the outbreak of the Civil War, but was rekindled in February 1905, when Brooklyn Controller Edward M. Grout called for a free public university. Grout's proposal for the borough to have its own college had its supporters, but there was opposition as well, both from the editor of *The New York Times* and from Nicholas Murray Butler, the powerful president of Columbia University. Their opposition helped to kill the necessary legislation proposed in the New York State Legislature in 1907.

A variety of options were explored to remedy the overcrowding at City and Hunter Colleges. In 1910, City College took the first step to ease the situation by responding to a request from the Brooklyn Teachers' Association and bringing to the borough (and later to Queens and the Bronx) extension courses for teachers, librarians, and social workers.

In 1917, an evening session for young men, administered by City College, opened at Boys' High School in Brooklyn, and Hunter started a similar program for women in the borough in 1924. Both Brooklyn programs offered only the first two years of college work. The Brooklyn Chamber of Commerce agreed in 1923 to support the idea of a college in Brooklyn, with its administration to be decided later. By 1925, the enrollment in the two evening sessions exceeded 2,000 students, establishing the borough as an alternative for those seeking publicly funded higher education. In the previous year *The New York Times* had published an article calling attention to the need for a free college in

Frederick B. Robinson, who later became president of City College, is shown in this picture lecturing to a class of women on the art of public speaking. The extension division of City College, which offered the course, began in 1910, and some of the college's most outstanding faculty members taught its classes. It conducted courses in the late afternoon and evening for teachers and librarians in the public schools—many of whom were women. *The New York Times* reported in September 1913 that the college's Department of Education had complete control over the courses: "Prof. Robinson presents another phase of the language in two courses on oral English and methods of teaching reading. Each course will extend over fifteen sessions. The first course presents two branches of oral English; the philosophy of expression and phonetics. The second course treats the history of reading methods and analysis of modern methods of teaching reading." *(City College Archives)*

Brooklyn, but only as a branch of City College. New York Supreme Court Justice Thomas Churchill, a City College graduate of 1882, expressed the sentiment of many alumni when he said:

> The congestion in the City College buildings here in Manhattan is steadily becoming worse. Hundreds of students are now being denied admission to City College solely because there is no room for them. The college is running day and night and now has a total registration of 23,000. The establishment of a Brooklyn branch would relieve much of this congestion. The new branch would have a real student body from the very start. There has been talk of starting an entirely new College in Brooklyn, but a college needs traditions. City College has been in existence about seventy-five years, which is old in this age.[2]

Frederick B. Robinson, a City College alumnus and by then its president, favored a separate college; the City College alumni continued to favor branch status for a four-year program in Brooklyn. With Robinson's assistance, legislation was drafted and finally passed in the New York State Legislature; Governor Alfred E. Smith signed it on April 16, 1926. The new act created a Board of Higher Education in New York City "to govern and administer that part of the public school system which is of collegiate grade and which leads to academic, technical and professional degrees."[3] The creation of one board to oversee the two existing colleges and any others that might be established later was intended to eliminate the need for multiple independent boards. When the new Board of Higher Education met for the first time on May 26, 1926, its first act was to establish the Brooklyn collegiate center in preparation for an envisioned four-year college. The City and Hunter boards conducted business until April 1926, when they dissolved themselves and the Board of Higher Education took up the administration of a corporation known as the College of the City of New York. Under the legislation, City College, Hunter College, Brooklyn College, and later Queens College were technically "centers" of this corporation, but they were actually separate undergraduate colleges with their own presidents and administrations and the freedom to develop their own curricula.

At the start of the twentieth century, when Brooklyn was attempting to establish a public college, New York City faced several other public education issues. Business education was an important addition to the curriculum at the turn of the century; however, New York City, the business center of the United States, offered only two business education programs at that time. One was instituted at New York University in 1900, and the other was established at a high school devoted to commerce, which opened in 1901. In addition, the College of the City of New York offered some nondegree business courses in the evening.

New York City was not alone in neglecting business education on the college level. In the nineteenth century, this subject area had been left to private "business colleges," which by the middle of the century were unable to meet the demand for highly trained workers. The public school system needed to become involved, and James A. Garfield, who was an educator before entering politics, promoted public sector support of business education. He felt that the rise of proprietary business colleges reflected the failure of the public schools to teach commercial subjects. Slowly, the idea of including business courses in the curricula took hold across the country. Toward the end of the nineteenth century, universities began to expand their programs, and in 1881 the prestigious Wharton School at the University of Pennsylvania admitted its first class. The first decades of the twentieth century witnessed a business education mania, mirroring President Coolidge's adage, "The business of America is business"; by 1925, there were 183 departments, schools, and courses in business in American colleges and universities.

The College of the City of New York tried various approaches to providing publicly supported business education. As early as 1871, a one-year commercial course was introduced, but both faculty (particularly those in classics) and students objected to it. The latter complained in the 1877–78 yearbook that the extreme youth of the commercial students "lowers the whole tone of the college," creating the impression that it was little more than a high school.[4] The program was modified and then dropped from the curriculum in 1881. The Normal College also tried to include business courses in the curriculum in the 1880s to help prepare teachers of business subjects, but similar faculty objections meant that they were not instituted until 1919 at the only recently renamed Hunter College.

The College of the City of New York reintroduced a few business courses through the Economics Division of its Department of Political Science in 1907,

The present-day building at 17 Lexington Avenue (now Baruch College) is on the site of the original Free Academy. After 1907, when the City College of New York moved to St. Nicholas Heights, the old Free Academy Building was still put to various uses, even though the city did not provide funds to repair the aged structure. However, once the new School of Business and Civic Administration opened its doors in the antiquated building in 1919, issues of safety and space once again became major concerns. Because the conditions were considered dangerous, the college's Board of Trustees consented to an inspection in 1923, but after a few fire violations were corrected, the building continued to function until 1926. Plans to construct a new building began in that year, but cost considerations led the Board of Estimate to rent facilities at Grand Central Palace on 42nd Street. This temporary location was unsatisfactory, however, and plans for an eight-story building proceeded. President Robinson and the Board of Trustees thought that a sixteen-story edifice would better serve the student population. The first eight floors were completed in September 1929, and the upper floors, which were finally approved by Mayor Walker, were finished in 1930. Townsend Harris Hall High School occupied the top three floors of the 1929 School of Business building from 1930 to 1942. *(Baruch College Archives)*

again generating interest in a business curriculum that culminated in the establishment of the School of Business and Civic Administration in 1919. Now students matriculating for the Bachelor of Business Administration degree (B.B.A.) were required to have a high school diploma and pursue a strong liberal arts core, including a foreign language, followed by the study of such specialized subjects as accountancy and business law. Rather than an awkward appendage with no relation to the rest of the curriculum, as the old commercial course had been, the B.B.A. was an integrated degree program with academic standing on a par with the B.A., B.S., engineering, and education degrees.

The Free Academy Building served as the first home of the School of Business and Civic Administration, but the old facility was inadequate, and under the sympathetic administration of Mayor James J. (Jimmy) Walker, funds were appropriated for a new building to replace it. Housed in its new skyscraper building, and with a curriculum ever alert to business and civic developments in the city, the School of Business rapidly attracted so many students to its day and evening programs that space issues arose again before the decade ended.

September 1926 was a landmark date for free higher education in Brooklyn, as the students of the future Brooklyn College began classes. There were two distinct units—the Brooklyn Collegiate Center of City College and the Brooklyn Collegiate Center of Hunter College. These centers quickly outgrew their leased quarters in downtown Brooklyn. The enrollment in 1926 was 623 men and 308 women. In the beginning, only the first two years of college could be completed at these satellite locations, and students had to travel to City College or Hunter College to complete their degrees.

The need for a permanent campus to accommodate a four-year college in the borough of Brooklyn was soon apparent, and a search was conducted for a suitable site. After a review of many proposals, the Board of Higher Education selected the Midwood "Wood-Harmon tract," former farmland and home to the Ringling Brothers and Barnum and Bailey Circus for many years. Brooklyn College was officially authorized on April 22, 1930, and opening ceremonies took place in September, although classes continued to operate at temporary locations in downtown Brooklyn. With the help of federal funds, construction of the neo-Georgian campus began in 1935, and in 1936 classes were held for the first time in the Midwood facility. The heritage of single-sex education did not immediately end at the new college. Men and women attended separate classes for required and lower division work; "co-education" was reserved for electives and upper division work, a situation that had less to do with educational philosophy than with economic realities. This separation of the college into the Men's Division and the Women's Division continued for more than a decade.

The debate over coeducation was not new. Nineteenth-century thinkers believed that the education of women would interfere with "maternity" and that the developmental differences of young men and young women warranted separate school facilities. Writing in the popular *Munsey's Magazine* in 1906, noted educator Dr. David Starr Jordan refuted the belief that coeducation adversely affects educational standards and deters women from marrying, saying: "It is of great advantage to both men and women to meet on a plane of equality in education."[5] It took decades, however, for this philosophy to become completely operative at New York's municipal colleges. City College established the first degree-granting evening session in the country in 1909, and within ten years it was admitting women. From

Opportunity Grows with the City 41

The location of a campus for Brooklyn College was a hotly debated issue. At one point, thirty different locations were under consideration. The Wood-Harmon tract, in an undeveloped area of Flatbush, seemed to possess particular advantages for a college campus—a residential environment and convenient transportation. In its prior life, it had served as a golf course and was also where Ringling Brothers and Barnum and Bailey Circus had pitched its tents.

The Board of Higher Education voted to acquire this property in December 1929, but the transaction did not go smoothly, and the Board of Estimate considered the price for the property too high. It was not until 1934 that New York City acquired title to the Wood-Harmon tract, providing a permanent home for Brooklyn College.
(Brooklyn College Archives)

1910, the Extension Division offered courses in the late afternoon and evening to teachers and librarians in the public schools—many of whom were women.

Not until 1930 could women enroll in day-session classes at the School of Business, and this victory was not easily won. Hunter College authorities opposed the admission of women in any day session classes created for men under the jurisdiction of the College of the City of New York. The Executive Committee of the Board of Higher Education passed a resolution on March 19, 1929, appointing a committee to make recommendations concerning the matter. Over the next year committees discussed the issue and made a recommendation to admit women to all technical and professional courses at the City College. In addition, the committee asserted that it was not passing judgment on coeducation, but was making the decision primarily to avoid duplication of facilities. However, a statement made by the committee was encouraging for women. "But this committee also concludes that women of the high school-graduate age or over, who purpose to pursue a business or professional career, need not be segregated as to sex in order to do their best work as students."[6] Women remained a minority in the City College day session classes until the 1940s.

The year 1926 was momentous in the borough's history. In May, the Board of Higher Education met and formed a Committee on Brooklyn Facilities to organize a Brooklyn center. The committee located temporary quarters, and Brooklyn's first full-time municipal institution conducting college-level classes began to educate Brooklyn students in September 1926.

In 1933, only seventeen women graduated from the School of Business, ten with diplomas and seven with the B.B.A. Even this meager number of women in attendance led to protests, and in 1933 women were again refused admittance into the day session programs. Morton Gottschall, acting dean of the College of Arts and Sciences at City College, justified the action on the basis of the need to restrict undergraduate enrollment and the recent introduction of business courses at Hunter College. *The New York Times* reported: "Dr. Gottschall pointed out that the City College courses were of little benefit to women students because they were not primarily designed for them. He cited the lack of secretarial training."[7] The 1933 decision was reversed in 1936 when Hunter College failed to develop a B.B.A. program of its own. Of the business class that entered in 1937, women made up one-tenth of the graduates—125 students. After Pearl Harbor, the composition of the entering classes at the School of Business changed. The majority of students during the war years were women, while postwar enrollments were fairly evenly balanced.

Hunter College, meanwhile, was attempting to expand other educational options for women. An article in *The New York Times* on May 8, 1927, headlined "Long Step Forward by Hunter College," highlighted the ceding by New York City of a thirty-acre section of the Jerome Park Reservoir site in the Bronx to the college. At that time it was predicted that construction would be completed in five years. The first of the Gothic Revival buildings was ready to receive students in September 1931, and the Works Progress Administration provided for the completion of the other three buildings in 1936. A fire at the Manhattan campus in 1936 led to the opening of a substantially larger Manhattan building in the fall of 1940, making the need for further new construction in the Bronx less urgent.

Opportunity Grows with the City 43

(Lehman College Archives)

In 1931, the Bronx Campus of Hunter College was established on thirty acres of land adjacent to the Jerome Park Reservoir. This campus originally offered the first two years of study to Hunter women, who then transferred to Hunter on Park Avenue. The early students were considered real pioneers, venturing to the yet undeveloped area of the Bronx to attend classes. A February 9, 1930, article in *The New York Times* reported that U.S. Attorney and Board of Higher Education member Charles H. Tuttle said of the Bronx: "We must look into the future . . . realizing as we do, that the Bronx is still a baby which hasn't started to grow yet." Construction of the campus proceeded slowly, and the first buildings were not completed until 1936. *(Courtesy of CUNY Office of Facilities Planning)*

The Bronx campus, after serving as a training center for the navy, reverted to collegiate instruction in October 1946. Now returning veterans joined the previously all-female student body, but they attended separate classes. True coeducation was not instituted until 1951, along with a four-year curriculum. The U.S. engagement in Korea, which began in 1950, precipitated the change because it presented the possibility of reduced enrollment in the day session of City College. After some debate, the Board of Higher Education passed a resolution allowing women to matriculate in the College of Liberal Arts and Sciences as of September 1951, while men were to be admitted in the same numbers to the Bronx Center of Hunter. The Board of Higher Education supplied a reason for this action. "[W]e would not want to find half of the seats at City College taken up by girls and then discover when the emergency no longer exists that we have deprived men students of more seats in the aggregate than we had provided for them at Hunter."[8] The tradition of single-sex education did not end completely at that time. Board chairman Ordway Tead noted, "[W]e leave the Hunter building at Park Avenue as a four-year college for girls exclusively, which seems a wise policy in order to take account of the desires of those families which may strongly prefer their daughters to go to a girls' college."[9] During the late 1940s and early 1950s, the size of the student body on the Bronx campus of Hunter remained constant at around 3,500.

Evening, summer, and extension division programs were added to the municipal college offerings early in the twentieth century. In addition, separate programs in business education and specialized courses for teachers and librarians expanded the options for students. The nondegree students at the School of Business were offered a variety of vocational and professional courses, including textiles, stenography, and typing. The Intensive Business Training Institute began after World War II. By 1947, it was located in a separate building on 50th Street, and noncredit courses in advertising, finance, and small-business management were taught until the program was terminated in 1955. "The success attained has come from matching up programs with the needs of this metropolitan area.... It is based on the advice and guidance of business leaders. It has utilized current surveys on the job opportunities and hence, training needs."[10] The business extension program established the School of Business as a partner with the New York business community, a relationship that has grown over the years.

The link between the municipal colleges and the New York City Police Department originated in the 1920s, when the Police Academy of New York City was organized into eight departments, including one for instructor training. An article in *The New York Times* on April 23, 1925, announced the opening of the Police Academy in the Commerce Building of the College of the City of New York (still housed in the old Free Academy Building) and stated that the college would help in planning new courses for the police school. "The Education School of the college will cooperate by conducting teachers' training courses for the instructors of the new school. This cooperation between two great departments of the city, one collegiate in character, the other the greatest police organization in the country and perhaps in the world, is most satisfactory and encouraging."[11] An in-service training course for prospective policemen began at the College of the City of New York in 1940. This two-year course included the study of sociology, psychology, criminal investigation, and principles of police administration. Courses for prospective policewomen were added in 1942, but America's deepening involvement in World War II led to the program's demise. It was not until the mid-1950s that the School of Business and the Police

The persevering evening students who earned their B.B.A. degrees in 1934 represented a range of ages and backgrounds. In 1932, the Board of Education, responding to a demand for access that exceeded the places conventionally available and desperate to control costs, created the status of "limited matriculants." These "second-tier" students, who could not meet the criteria for full, tuition-free matriculation, were considered competent but lacked the high school records that qualified them for admission to a degree program. They were admitted to the evening session as nondegree students on a fee-paying basis (originally about $2.50 per credit). The colleges developed methods for these students to gain matriculated status. City College first required them to earn a B average in a minimum of fifteen credits over two consecutive terms; in 1941, transfer became possible with a C average for sixty completed credits. The other colleges crafted similar policies. In 1941, Brooklyn College developed associate degree programs conducted entirely in the evening. Transfer programs between day and evening sessions, and between the community and four-year colleges, emerged in the 1950s and 1960s, allowing "second tier" students to earn their way academically to matriculated, free-tuition status at the senior colleges.

The senior and community colleges also developed a variety of new programs for those who were not seeking a degree. City College's School of Business created an extensive program of short nondegree courses in the practical aspects of running all types of small businesses. This Intensive Business Training Institute was originally designed for veterans, but its popularity led to offerings for the general public. The institute, which operated until 1955, was a revenue producer for the school. The St. Nicholas Heights campus of City College established a low-cost program of short nondegree courses in arts and crafts, foreign languages, English language instruction, and business subjects. The New York Public Library branch system provided the facilities, which allowed these courses to be offered throughout Manhattan, the Bronx, and Staten Island between 1944 and 1966.

Today, CUNY campuses offer evening classwork toward degrees, continuing education programs, and work toward the General Educational Development (GED) diploma. All over New York City, from Lehman in the northern Bronx to Kingsborough in south Brooklyn, from Queensborough in eastern Queens to John Jay on the far west side of Manhattan, learners keep the campuses aglow at night. *(Baruch College Archives)*

Academy merged their efforts in a degree-granting program. In 1955, a new Police Academy building was in the planning stages and was slated to include teaching facilities on the Lexington Avenue campus (renamed the Bernard M. Baruch School of Business and Public Administration in 1953). The commander of the Academy was to serve as the assistant dean of police studies. However, the final plan authorized the Police Academy to be used solely for police training, and in 1965 the programs were removed from what was now renamed Baruch College and transferred to a new College of Police Science.

By 1930 Brooklyn had its own college and the Bronx had the uptown campus of Hunter College, but Queens did not get a four-year municipal college until 1937. Public higher education first came to Queens in 1924, when City College established a Queens Center on the top floor of William Cullen Bryant High School, then in Long Island City. This center offered the first two years of college work and was coeducational except for physical education. From the beginning, women were an integral part of the Queens Center, participating actively in athletics, student government, journalism, and dramatics. At the same time, the Board of Higher Education's ambivalence about coeducation manifested itself in the early policy at Brooklyn College and in the creation of a freshman year program for men that City College ran at James Monroe High School in the Bronx between 1933 and 1936.

In 1935 Judge Charles S. Colden mobilized a citizen drive and then formed the Committee for a Queens Free College. At the end of 1936, Mayor Fiorello LaGuardia agreed to establish the college on the site of the discontinued New York Parental School in Flushing. *The New York Times* reported: "The Board of Higher Education, meeting last night at the School of Business of City College, Lexington

President Frederick Robinson of City College is shown presiding over the first class in English at the Police Academy in New York City in 1933. The courses were designed to advance police work and enable members of the department "to discourse creditably on matters of police activity." *(CUNY Central Office Archives/Corbis Images)*

Avenue and Twenty-third Street, approved proposals to establish a Queens branch of City College in twelve buildings of the Parental School on Parsons Boulevard in Flushing, now under the jurisdiction of the Department of Hospitals."[12]

The Board of Higher Education appointed Dr. Paul Klapper of City College to lead the new school, and from the beginning his ambitions were high: "We must build more than a college for young people; we must develop a great cultural center for the Borough of Queens."[13] Klapper was a 1904 graduate of City College and had organized, taught in, and administered its School of Education. He personally chose the first sixty faculty and staff members, searching for excellence in teaching as well as scholarship. He designed a curriculum that required substantial study of literature, social studies, art, and music, along with two semesters of composition. The first freshman class in 1937 had 400 students. By 1943, the student body exceeded 1,500.

With the establishment of Queens College, all the boroughs of New York City had the advantages of a free municipal college, except Staten Island. This outer borough would not get its own college until the 1950s. Before that could happen, the community college movement had to reach New York City, attracting students who traditionally did not have the opportunity to obtain a higher education.

The two-year junior college in America dates from early in the twentieth century. The concept is rooted both in the need for properly trained technical workers and in the emergent belief that adolescents still required custodial care and more education. Public and private junior colleges (which came to be known as community colleges in the 1940s) were first established in 1920, along with junior college departments in high schools. During the Depression of the 1930s

Queens College opened on October 3, 1937, on the former site of the New York Parental School in Flushing. The buildings, which were to remain in use into the 1960s, were considered temporary and did not include any theater or auditorium that could be used for the institution's first commencement. *The New York Times* reported in June 1941: "While drenching rains fell, under the doubtful protection of a carnival tent, 198 members of the first class to enter Queens College yesterday afternoon received their bachelor degrees, becoming the first graduates of the four-year-old institution, at commencement exercises on the campus of the college, 65-30 Kissena Boulevard." Mayor LaGuardia addressed the 3,000 people in attendance at this landmark event for the borough of Queens, outlining the role of the college graduate during the wartime crisis. Dr. Walter A. Jessup, the president of the Carnegie Foundation for the Advancement of Teaching, gave the baccalaureate speech. *(City College Archives)*

these institutions became even more important, as they offered training programs and opportunities to retrain the unemployed.

New York was slow to embrace the idea of the two-year college, although during the 1920s and 1930s the New York State Department of Education saw the need to train students in technical skills after high school graduation. However, World War II further demonstrated the importance of technical education, and the community college movement gained broader public awareness.

In 1940, Brooklyn College recommended the establishment of a two-year curriculum leading to the Associate in Arts degree and other two-year terminal vocational programs. Albany did not approve the associate's degree, but Brooklyn College decided to offer the programs first and wait for approval later. This took a decade, and Brooklyn eventually phased out its two-year degree programs.

During World War II, educational institutions established emergency programs to teach the skills needed in the war effort. On December 13, 1943, the New York City Board of Education passed a resolution requesting that the Board of Regents set up a two-year State Institute of Technical and Applied Arts after the war. The Regents approved the plan, and a Temporary State Commission on Institutes was created in 1945. On April 4, 1946, the governor and legislature authorized five institutes, one of which was to be located in New York City. The New York Institute of Applied Arts and Sciences was established in 1946, and on February 5, 1947, the first classes were held at Public School 15 on Schermerhorn Street and Third Avenue in Brooklyn.

The State University of New York was formed in 1948 with authority to develop two-year community colleges throughout the state. The Board of Higher Education commissioned education planner Donald P. Cottrell to lead a team that would develop a master plan. This plan was issued in 1950 under the title *Public Higher Education in the City of New York*. The Cottrell report recommended that community colleges be established in all boroughs except Manhattan. State law was altered in 1952 to allow the Board of Higher Education to sponsor such colleges, and in 1953 the New York Institute of Applied Arts and Sciences became New York City Community College, now the four-year New York City Technical College.

Staten Island was thus the only borough without a municipal college. For two decades, its residents had conducted letter-writing campaigns to community leaders, in which hundreds of Staten Island mothers asked that their children have the same opportunity for free higher education that was available to students living in the other four boroughs. This dream was finally realized in 1956 with the opening of a community college in the St. George section of the island. Although other two-year programs were already in place, they had not been under the jurisdiction of the Board of Higher Education.

Community colleges in New York City were becoming an essential way to meet the increased demand for admission to the municipal colleges. Bronx community leaders now began to fight to establish a community college in their borough. Mayor Robert F. Wagner received many letters and petitions from Bronx citizens requesting the formation of such an institution. In 1956, Board of Higher Education Chairman Dr. Joseph Cavallaro said: "I am strongly encouraged that we will succeed in the establishment of a greatly needed community college in the Bronx."[14]

Bronx Community College was founded in 1957, with prominent educator Dr. Morris Meister as its first president. It officially opened in February 1959 with the admission of its first class of 123 students. After years of being housed in an assortment of

The first location of the New York State Institute of Applied Arts and Sciences (forerunner of New York City Technical College) was on Schermerhorn Street and 3rd Avenue in Brooklyn, former home of Public School 15. The class entering on February 5, 1947, studied both academic and general education subjects. Otto Klitgord, who was named the first director of the institute, emphasized that the purpose of the school was to train both men and women to work in business and industry at the technical and subprofessional levels. The initial courses covered a variety of occupational fields such as communication and electrical technology. Commercial art, industrial design, and dental technology, to name just a few, were added several months later.

The Schermerhorn location was far from ideal, and 300 Pearl Street was to be the next home of the Institute. The institute was an independently operated public college for ten years. On July 1, 1957, sponsorship of the institute was transferred to New York City, and the name was changed to New York City Community College. The community college movement had already begun in New York City with the opening of Staten Island Community College in 1956, and additional community colleges were soon to follow in the Bronx and Queens. (*CUNY Central Office Archives*)

As early as 1938, Staten Island residents petitioned the Board of Higher Education to establish a college in Staten Island. They based their case on the difficult commute faced by students who wanted to enroll at municipal colleges, as well as on the projected growth of the high school population in the borough. Residents continued to express their concerns in letter-writing campaigns into the 1940s.

In response to this effort, the Board of Higher Education recommended that a center be established in the borough in rented quarters, which would be under the control of Queens College; however, this center never materialized. A September 17, 1956, ceremony at Borough Hall Plaza marked the occasion when Staten Island residents finally got their community college.

rented buildings, the college got a real campus in 1973. It relocated to the former University Heights campus of New York University, which includes buildings designed by Stanford White as well as the Hall of Fame of Great Americans.

In 1958, the Board of Higher Education estimated that the number of New York State high school graduates would increase from 115,191 to 242,000 in the period from 1955 to 1970. Technical education was growing in popularity, and community colleges were one way to address the enrollment problem. *The New York Times* reported: "In approving a two-year community college for Queens the Board of Estimate has taken a necessary step to help alleviate a growing shortage of higher education facilities in this city. The Queens Community College will help hundreds of qualified boys and girls attain a low-cost education and the city will have a community college in each of its five boroughs as a result of the Board of Estimate's action."[15] Expansion plans for the new school were ambitious. An entering class of 400 was expected to increase to 4,000 within a few years.

As with most of the other municipal colleges, Queensborough Community College began in temporary quarters. Students, faculty, and administrators occupied trailers and Quonset huts during these pioneer days, and the first group of permanent buildings opened in Bayside, Queens, in 1967. Queensborough Community College brought a broader range of higher education choices to the residents of Queens.

Public higher education in New York City came a long way between the end of World War I and 1960. The number of colleges increased, coeducation became a reality, and business education took its rightful place in the curriculum. The community college movement helped to broaden preprofessional and technical education opportunities and, through transfer programs, provided another route for admission into four-year colleges. Politicians and educators thus showed themselves to be increasingly responsive to the needs of their communities.

By the end of 1960, New York City was feeling the effect of a number of political, economic, and social developments that would have an impact on public higher education in the coming decade. Although the city's population declined from 7,891,957 in 1950 to 7,781,984 by 1960, a new wave of immigrants arrived in the 1950s. The number of high school students wanting to attend college increased. Puerto Ricans and African Americans from the south came in sizable numbers, augmenting their long-established communities in New York. The Hungarian uprising of 1956 and the Cuban revolution of 1959 also brought new immigrants to the city. These people were the new aspirants for educational advancement, but the city's economic base was changing, and for those without

As did Staten Island residents, Bronx community groups also urged the Board of Higher Education to establish a community college in their borough in the late 1940s. Unfortunately, this initial interest died out until Bronx Borough President James J. Lyons revived the plan for a community college in the borough. Despite having its own Bronx Campus at the time, New York University was not concerned about competition from a community college. The scene was set to approve a proposal made to the Board of Estimate by the borough presidents of the Bronx and Queens to establish community colleges in their respective boroughs. The decision to establish a community college in the Bronx was made in 1957, but it did not enroll its first students until 1959. Located in several different buildings in the Bronx over the years, the college moved to its present location on the University Heights campus in 1973.

Today Bronx Community College is known for its programs in the health sciences, business, and public service, and it is actively involved with the community through extension courses, evening and Saturday programs, and special programs for the elderly, children, the disabled, and veterans. The business community also benefits from programs offered by the Bronx Community College; the Business and Professional Development Institute was established ten years ago, and a Small Business Development Center opened on campus in 1994. *(Bronx Community College)*

Bernard M. Baruch, class of 1889, maintained a close relationship with his alma mater throughout his life. Contributing substantial gifts to the school, he was recognized as an inspiration for students and a promoter of Americanism. The School of Business and Civic Administration of the College of the City of New York was renamed the Bernard M. Baruch School of Business and Public Administration. Ceremonies marking the name change and honoring this "true American" took place on October 8, 1953. *(Baruch College Archives)*

Women are shown in a secretarial class at Bernard M. Baruch School of Business and Public Administration in 1955. *(Baruch College Archives)*

education and skills, the American dream of upward mobility and increased prosperity was becoming harder to achieve. Well-paying unskilled jobs began to leave the city, replaced by those requiring a liberal arts or technical education, and making the plight of many of the new arrivals and their families more difficult. The unfortunate economic status of these new minorities led to a major change in municipal higher education in New York City.

The City University of New York, formed in 1961, federated the senior and community colleges into one system. While a driving force behind its creation was the need to provide publicly supported doctoral work, the university would soon confront the inescapable challenge of the need to serve all New Yorkers who aspired to transform their lives through public higher education.

Notes

1. Hood, *733 Miles*, 101.
2. *The New York Times* (October 19, 1924), 29.
3. New York (State). *Education Law. Article 44-A, sec. 1142*, April 16, 1926.
4. *CCNY Microcosm, 1877–78*, 708.
5. Jordan, "The Question of Coeducation," 684.
6. New York (N.Y.) Board of Higher Education. "Minutes of Proceedings, January 21, 1930," 60–63.
7. "City College Ban Is Put on Women," *The New York Times* (May 26, 1933), 21.
8. New York (N.Y.). Board of Higher Education. *Minutes*, 1951, 5.
9. Ibid., 5.
10. Love, "New Friends for City College," 9.
11. "City College Is Ready for Police Academy," *The New York Times* (April 23, 1925), 11.
12. "Queens City College Is Favored by Board," *The New York Times* (April 15, 1936), 11
13. "Dr. Klapper Heads Queens College," *The New York Times* (May 26, 1937), 23.
14. New York (N.Y.) Board of Higher Education. "Minutes of Proceedings, September 24, 1956," S-27.
15. "Community College for Queens," *The New York Times* (July 3, 1958), 24.

4 Student Life at "Subway Schools"

James Renwick's design for the Free Academy Building did not include space for student activities. The nonresidential character of the academy, coupled with the youth of the students, led most faculty to disapprove of student activities within the school walls. Until the late nineteenth century, even administrators at residential colleges did not concern themselves with student social activities. The "extra-curriculum" was not part of the academic program of the college, and many felt it was actually in opposition to it. Nevertheless, academy students then, like students today, creatively sought ways to socialize and organize. Corridors, alcoves, and staircase landings quickly became the sites of informal meetings between classes. While student life at CUNY today is far richer and more varied than it was in the nineteenth century, such important activities as publications, athletics, and social and special interest clubs quickly took root at the Free Academy. When the Normal College (Hunter College) was established in 1869, its women also created their own student traditions.

Extracurricular activities helped Normal College students master the skills of leadership and management useful to women who often had to earn their own living. By the early 1900s, women at Hunter were running for class office and participating in athletics. The practice that graduates received by engaging in these activities, when added to their baccalaureate degree, allowed them to pursue careers in the professions as well as teaching in the public schools and colleges.

Hunter and City College students participated in secret societies, fraternities, and sororities and brought energy and enthusiasm to publications and athletic teams. As the decades passed, students with professional ambitions created societies in law, engineering, medicine, and the like, and those interested primarily in the arts or in politics founded their own formal and informal groups.

Student literary and debating societies emerged at American colleges in the 1730s. They became a setting in which students could pursue self-cultivation and master the skills of writing, speaking, and debating. Events at the young Free Academy reflected this tradition, and two societies were founded—Clionia in the fall of 1851 and Phrenocosmia in 1852. By 1851, six entering classes (those of February and September) had been admitted, creating a student body of several hundred. "With a free field, without traditions, without precedent or experience to guide them, with no bond of union between the different classes, the students conceived the idea that the classes could be best united and a college sentiment developed by the foundation of a literary society constituted of the members of all classes."[1]

At first, Clionia held its evening meetings at P.S. 35 on 13th Street, where Dr. Thomas Hunter, then the

Student Life 55

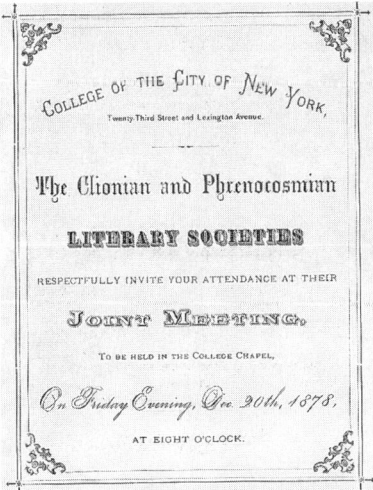

Clionia members were particularly proud of their library, which reflected their privileged status at City College. Students used the library as a place to gather informally, prepare debates, and read books such as *Tom Jones* and *The Decameron*, which were definitely not included in the college curriculum. Their motto, "We fight as brothers," suggests their closeness to one another and their fierce rivalry with the other literary and debating society, Phrenocosmia. For its members, student life revolved around Clionia, and they did not join other groups. Phrenocosmia members, on the other hand, tended to have wider collegiate interests. Felix Frankfurter, class of 1902 and a future associate justice of the U.S. Supreme Court, was a member of Clionia. *(City College Archives)*

principal, permitted the group to use a classroom. These candlelight meetings ended several months later when President Webster allowed groups to meet in the Academy after class hours. Initially both Clionia and Phrenocosmia held debates among their own members. In 1859, however, they began the custom of holding joint debates, which lasted until the start of World War I. While both groups published journals—somewhat irregularly—their major activity was the joint debates, which were held in rented halls several times a year. Although athletics are the most widely recognized competitive element of student life, debating societies and the school newspapers of the nineteenth century served as preparation for life in that era's competitive, capitalist society.

Fraternities and secret societies jealously guarded their spaces, just as students of the next century commandeered tables for their Greek letter societies and House Plans in cafeterias and student unions. By 1859, the fraternities and literary societies controlled the yearbook and the elections for student orators. The majority of students who did not belong to these organizations formed a temporary alliance, the Manhattan League, to challenge this dominance. Charging the fraternity men with arrogance and oppression, the league attracted a large membership, but it disbanded once it succeeded in curbing the abuses of the societies. Fraternities never again dominated student life at City College, although Greek life flourished at other campuses of the expanding City University system through the 1960s.

While Clionia and Phrenocosmia had the approval of the administration, conflict arose in 1854 when the board attempted to assert control over their activities by ordering the groups to hold daytime meetings, to exclude first-year students or "sub-freshmen," and to disband their libraries. Although all of these regulations were met with dismay, the students were particularly upset by the order to disband their libraries, as the college library was open only one-half-hour a week at the time. Rather than comply, the students rented off-campus space for their meetings. This tactic evidently caused the board to reconsider, and in 1857 the students were even allowed to establish libraries in small rooms adjoining the top-floor chapel. Although all faculty members were ex-officio members of the societies, in practice the students appeared to run them without faculty involvement or interference. This episode marked the first time that the students contested an administrative attempt to control the way they ran their organizations.

The nineteenth-century Normal College was a serious institution. President Thomas Hunter did not support most extracurricular activities, but he did believe that literary societies were a means to intellectual improvement, not just frivolous clubs. The Philomathean and Alpha Beta Gamma literary societies, whose establishment he approved in 1870, remained popular into the twentieth century, when their members celebrated holidays with special musical and dramatic programs. At the turn of the century, new literary societies were formed, and fourteen were listed in the student magazine of 1900. Intramural debating was in vogue in 1891, when Normal College women held their first contest. While interest in debating waned after several years, glee clubs, birding and botany clubs, religious clubs, and drama and mandolin clubs thrived on East 68th Street.

Fraternities have been part of student life in New York since 1825, where they originated as a reaction against student revolts that broke out on residential campuses following the American Revolution. These uprisings pitted students against faculties, with their patriarchal discipline and their refusal to listen to student complaints. Students of the 1820s tired of the pattern of petitions, revolts, suspensions, and apologies. Instead, they adopted the tactic of creating secret organizations that would exist apart from the faculty, and in which they could set their own rules. Fraternities became the foundation of the "extra-curriculum," which made college for some students "a little space of time . . . where the young made a world to suit themselves."[2] The fact that students lived at home and often had to work part time hindered fraternity life at the Free Academy. On the majority of residential campuses, most day students were viewed as outsiders, but such elitism had no place at the Free Academy. By 1866, the academy had four chapters of national fraternities, and they instituted rushing. A City College graduate of the class of 1872 suggested that fraternities offered the students a badly needed opportunity to establish close friendships at a college whose enrollment then numbered about 1,000.

Hunter women also yearned to participate in Greek life and established chapters of several sororities, which were eventually linked in a Pan-Hellenic Association that coordinated them. However, sororities were expensive and excluded women of modest means.

"Secret societies," whose memberships were generally limited to a single class, were in fashion at many colleges during the nineteenth century, including City College. They featured secret handshakes, cryptic

President Hunter was not an advocate of "extra-curricular" activities, and he did not promote the formation of clubs by the Normal College women. However, he did give his consent to the creation of the Philomathean and Alpha Beta Gamma literary societies in the 1870s, believing that membership might be a way for the women to improve their minds. *(Hunter College Archives)*

When Richard Rogers Bowker died in 1933 at the age of 85, a long obituary in the *City College Alumnus* stressed his lifelong empathy with the problems and ideals of students. Coming to the college in 1863 when it was still the Free Academy, Bowker was ardent in both his love for the school and his desire to improve it. In addition to launching *The Collegian* magazine, in 1866 he pioneered the establishment of the first democratically elected student council on any American college campus. This early venture in student self-government aggravated President Horace Webster, with his West Point views.

Bowker showed further initiative the next year when he secured a chapter of Phi Beta Kappa, the national scholastic honor society, for City College. A chapter had been requested in the Free Academy days but was refused, evidently on the grounds that the institution's collegiate status was not clear. Once that status, which had been officially conferred by the state legislature in 1853, was ratified by the change of name to the College of the City of New York in 1866, Bowker approached the New York Alpha Chapter of Phi Beta Kappa at Union College in Schenectady. After examining the college's claim, Alpha granted the Gamma Chapter to City College in 1867. President Webster was elected the first president of the chapter. Unfortunately for Bowker, his clash with Webster over the student government issue caused Webster to blackball him when he came up for election. Though Bowker refused later offers of membership, he never faltered in his love and work for the college, even during a long career in publishing and politics. *(City College Archives)*

Student Life 59

Nineteenth-century graduating classes at City College generally contained about 40 students out of the 350 who entered as "sub-freshmen." Class members knew each other well by their senior year and developed a rich tradition of class dinners. Elaborately printed menus accompanied a program of songs, toasts, and reminiscences. This dinner, held at Sieghortner's Restaurant on May 4, 1883, was the tenth for the class of 1877, which, rather unusually, began its class dinner tradition in the freshman year. The 1883 dinner featured several courses, which were expected at nineteenth-century banquets, as well as convivial toasts and speeches. *(City College Archives)*

insignia, and hints of innocently wicked rituals. The E.Z.O.X. society was represented in the 1874–75 yearbook with an emblem that showed an emaciated student buying peanuts from an organ grinder.

By the late 1950s, City College had more than forty active fraternities and sororities, whose activities were coordinated by an Inter-Fraternity Council. The council broadened Greek life to include activities other than the traditional fraternity parties by sponsoring distinguished speakers, intramural sports, community service activities, and a newspaper. A faculty member in the student life department at Brooklyn College wrote that the Greeks "offer their members the advantages of belonging to a social group which gives some security in the immensity of the Brooklyn College campus."[3] The daytime enrollment at Brooklyn College was then about 10,000. In the 1970s interest in Greek life diminished at CUNY, as it did on campuses all over the country. Signs of revival have now appeared at a few CUNY campuses, but the current fraternities operate without the structure and range of activities made possible by the council system during their heyday.

By the 1930s, the City College student body had grown far beyond the projected capacity of the 1907 campus. Classes were in session from 8:00 A.M. until 11:00 P.M. Only a small fraction of the student body was involved in student government and varsity teams. The activities of the academic and special interest clubs were limited by the system's insistence on club hours (i.e., special times devoted to club activities). In 1934, under the leadership of Mortimer Karpp, freshman advisor to the class of 1938, City College pioneered House Plan, or Student Houses. House Plan was designed to bring to City College some of the advantages of living in small groups enjoyed by students at residential colleges such as Harvard and Yale. The founders did not envision House Plan as merely an

The evening session of City College admitted women more than thirty-five years before they were able to matriculate in the day session's College of Liberal Arts and Sciences. The "girls" shown in this 1926 photograph were ambitious pioneers in what was basically a man's world. "Main Branch" refers to the St. Nicholas Heights campus. The School of Business was more informally known uptown as 23rd Street. *(City College Archives)*

extracurricular activity but rather as "cocurricular"—an integral part of the educational process. Any student could participate in House Plan. Its administrators would create a new house to accommodate groups of between twelve and twenty students who wanted to belong. Students at the School of Business wasted little time lobbying for space for their House Plan Association. In 1936, they occupied a building at 138 Lexington Avenue, and in the fall of 1943, the Lamport Foundation gave the school the building at 25 East 22nd Street, which was partially supported by the donor and partially by student fees paid to the House Plan Association. The individual houses sponsored parties, and a Council of Student Delegates ran the general program of teas, dances, athletic competitions, trips, and cultural activities. Faculty were invited to participate in all of these activities, and a number did so.

House Plan came to Brooklyn College in 1936 and to Hunter College the next year. Starting in 1939, City College House Plan developed Carnival as the major activity in which all groups participated. At Brooklyn, the House Plans played a major role in the annual Country Fair. By the mid-1950s, more than 2,000 students were actively involved in one hundred houses at City College. The House Plan Association also published a regular paper, *Megathon*; the Brooklyn College equivalent was *Calling Card*. The originators of House Plan had tried not only to create opportunities for college friendships but also to help students improve their "social skills." After World War II, this concern blossomed in the "human relations" weekends that became a hallmark of House Plans.

As the House Plan movement spread, it retained the inclusiveness that was its original purpose. A faculty member at New York City Technical College recalled how House Plan was established there in the late 1940s (when it was still a community college): "House Plans were a big social feature. They were a

Student Life 61

For some members, the heart of House Plan was the individual house parties such as this one held at City College about 1940, with women guests invited from Hunter. In 1935, shortly after House Plan was established, a niece of Edward Morse Shepard, class of 1869, gave the organization a granite townhouse at 292 Convent Avenue, just north of the college, and another one was acquired soon thereafter. Shepard House gave students a place to plan their intramural activities and carnivals, learn to cook, and participate in the Monopoly craze of the 1930s. Eleanor Roosevelt visited the houses and complimented the organization on its goals and activities. In 1955, City College opened its first student union, a renovated building on the recently acquired property south of 135th Street, and House Plan moved to the John H. Finley Student Center. House Plans at Brooklyn College frequently rented and decorated spaces in homes near the campus. *(City College Archives)*

Brooklyn College celebrated its "birthday" each May between 1938 and 1968 with a Country Fair, which involved every campus group. Each organization, singly or cooperatively, prepared an event or attraction. As the college grew, so did the fair. Eventually it offered sporting events, a water ballet, a carousel, and a hayride, as well as food, square dancing, music, and the chance to win prizes at games of skill. The fair, run entirely by students, became a popular neighborhood event for families, friends, and neighbors of the college and even included an evening barn dance. By the mid-1950s, it received a budget of $15,000. A sizable profit was realized from these start-up funds; this profit was used for scholarships and other programs that directly benefited student life. During the fair's first two decades, when the Faculty Wives Club flourished, this group raised money for the Student Loan Fund by selling donated merchandise at its fair booth. Adele Bildersee, the college's first dean of women, made the Country Fair a special interest, believing strongly that students thrived if they made personal contacts at the college. (*Brooklyn College Archives*)

Student Life **63**

Hazing, imposed on freshmen by sophomores, has been characterized as a process of acculturation for first-year male students. It generally involved rules of deferential behavior toward the "sophs," which the frosh ignored at their peril. Student life at the nonresidential campuses of CUNY was free of the particularly vicious forms of hazing that characterized some residential campuses. Nevertheless, City College officially discontinued the practice in the 1920s. In the 1930s, the prescriptive "rules" of earlier decades designed to keep freshmen in a suitable state of lowliness gradually gave way to handbooks intended to be friendly guides.

variation of what in another college would be called a fraternity. But at our place, anyone who cared to belong was able to. House Plans were not as exclusive as fraternities or sororities."[4] House Plans were also operating at the Borough of Manhattan Community College, Queensborough Community College, and Queens College.

Despite the success of House Plans, the problem of a lack of adequate social facilities for students at the colleges was not totally resolved. In 1907, City College's main building had a dingy "student concourse," which by the 1930s had become severely overcrowded and had few facilities. Alumni fund-raising in the late 1920s, however, was devoted to construction of a new library, not to enhancing student life. The Brooklyn College campus of 1937, a product of careful design, did not include a student union, and one was not added until 1962. When Queens College took over the existing facilities of the failed Parental School in 1937, it did not allocate any space to student activities.

While setting aside space for a formal student union was not in the immediate future, by the mid-1940s funds were made available to enable the School of Business of City College to establish Lamport House for student activities. However, a variety of extracurricular activities continued at 17 Lexington Avenue, where the Department of Student Life was housed. In 1957, the school acquired the Family Court building on 22nd Street, opening it as the new student center in 1960. Hunter College obtained Roosevelt House, the East Side home where Sara Delano Roosevelt raised her son Franklin. The house, dedicated on November 23, 1943, served as a social center for Hunter students and their families, alumnae, and faculty for more than forty years. Teas became a weekly event, and the student life staff coordinated programs of dances, lectures, and concerts. In the early 1990s, such activities were relocated to Thomas Hunter Hall on 68th Street and Lexington Avenue. This Gothic Revival building, erected in 1912 as part of Hunter College, is the only portion to have survived the fire of 1936. It housed Hunter College High School until the early 1970s.

City University of New York students have created a rich and varied club life. The large number of clubs offers students opportunities to share common interests, learn to plan programs, and request and manage budgets. At City College alone, several hundred clubs have flourished since the establishment of Clionia in 1851. In the 1890s, these included mandolin and chess clubs as well as musical societies, a golf club, and a camera club. The Dramatic Society was established in 1887 by James K. Hackett of the class of 1891, who went on to become an internationally acclaimed Shakespearean actor. Over time it evolved into "DramSoc," which from 1945 to 1974 produced at least two shows annually.

The City College "lunchroom" of the 1930s in the basement of Shepard Hall featured a counter that provided a very limited selection of food (although many students brought their own lunches) and chest-high wooden tables. In the early 1930s, a mezzanine level was installed to house student clubs, which lowered the lunchroom ceiling and made the room very noisy. A Ping-Pong table provided excitement. A wide aisle was broken into alcoves. Each alcove contained built-in benches and long tables that were gathering places for various campus groups, including athletes, African American students, and members of religious organizations.

Alcoves 1 and 2 were home to the anti-Stalinist and pro-Stalinist left, respectively. Irving Kristol of the class of 1940 emerged in the 1970s as a leader of the neoconservative movement. In the 1930s, he was a habitue of Alcove 1, and his 1977 essay, "Memoirs of a Trotskyite," examined his radical past at City College.

[B]eing a young radical was not simply part of my college experience; it was practically the whole of it. If I left City College with a better education than did many students at other and supposedly better colleges, it was because my involvement in radical politics put me in touch with people and ideas that prompted me to read and think and argue with a furious energy. . . . Going to City College meant, for me, being a member of this group. It was a privileged experience, and I know of no one who participated in it who does not look back upon it with some such sentiment.

Irving Howe, who would retain his socialist sympathies, also devoted part of his memoir, *A Margin of Hope,* to the alcove scene, describing its "thick brown darkness," where "we educated and mis-educated ourselves. Anyone could join in an argument, there was no external snobbism; but whoever joined did so at his own risk, fools and ignoramuses, not being suffered gladly." Other alcove regulars were Daniel Bell, Seymour Martin Lipset, and Melvin Lasky. The regulars of Alcoves 1 and 2 numbered perhaps 150 out of a student body of several thousand, but they have come to represent City College in the 1930s. Alcove 1, Kristol's choice, was home not only to Trotskyites, but also to what he called "grouplets": "right-wing" socialists, "Norman Thomas socialists," and adherents of other leftist theoreticians who styled themselves Lovestoneites, Ohlerites, and Marlinites. Participation in the life of the political alcoves promoted extensive reading in the social sciences and in *Partisan Review,* the political and intellectual journal of the anti-Stalinist left, edited by City College graduate William Phillips of the class of 1928.

The lunchroom was remodeled late in 1941, and tables with chairs were provided for all. Many of the most devoted alcovites had graduated, and soon World War II would claim many more. But for a decade, the college's most politically aware students spent all their free time in Alcoves 1 and 2, where, as Kristol recalled in 1977, "one argued incessantly, and generally devoted oneself to solving the ultimate problems of the human race. The penultimate problems we figured could be left for our declining years, after we had graduated."
(City College Archives)

City College was one of the first colleges in the nation to offer courses in radio engineering, and a student Radio Club was established in 1922. The Amateur Radio Club was formed after World War II, and in 1955 the Beaver Broadcasters were organized. Other campuses followed suit, including Brooklyn College, which had an active radio club. Today almost every unit of the City University of New York operates a radio station.

All campuses maintain clubs focusing on avocational interests. Those that have come and gone on various campuses over time include bridge clubs, veterans' clubs, the Eugene V. Debs Club, the Ayn Rand Club, and folk song clubs. In the 1960s, performances of the Ballad Club at New York City Technical College revealed a number of talented singers and guitar players among the student body. Soon after the first class of 537 young men and women entered LaGuardia Community College in 1971, the students established organizations reflecting their various affinities. Over the years, these have included accounting, Asian music, literary, theater, and law clubs. The Haitian and Bangladesh clubs, open to all students, reflect the diversity of the campus and the desire of students to share their culture. Despite the challenges of commuting, employment, and family responsibilities, CUNY students continue to create and participate in campus clubs.

Organizations that bring together students with shared religious beliefs date back to the mid-1860s, when a small group of Free Academy students received permission to meet on Friday afternoons in a basement classroom as the City College Christian Association. When the Young Men's Christian Association established its headquarters near the college in 1868, members of the City College Christian Association joined in its social activities, and it eventually became an intercollegiate branch of the YMCA.

(By permission of Esquire Magazine. Hearst Communications, Inc. Esquire is a trademark of Hearst Magazines Property, Inc. All rights reserved.)

(New York City Technical College Archive)

In the student culture of dances, proms, and carnivals that flourished between the end of World War II and the mid-1960s, the campus queen held sway. Chosen by vote, she was crowned and laden with flowers at a climactic social event. The young woman shown seated and holding a bouquet was chosen as the prom queen at New York City Community College (now New York City Technical College) in 1968.

The first student organization for Roman Catholics to adopt the name Newman Club was formed at the University of Pennsylvania in 1893. In 1915, the Newman Club at City College joined with other Roman Catholic student clubs in the metropolitan area, including the Barat Club at Hunter College, to form the Federation of Catholic College Clubs. Fostering the spiritual and theological growth of the membership, the Newman Clubs at the municipal colleges sponsored intellectual and cultural programs intended to appeal to the entire student body. Participation in Newman Club activities after World War II was so strong that, by the mid-1950s, the Diocese of Brooklyn assigned one priest to full-time duties as chaplain of the Newman Clubs at Brooklyn and Queens Colleges.

The Jewish students who attended City College and the Normal College up to 1890 generally came from families who had emigrated from Western Europe, particularly Germany, and who had rapidly become acculturated into life in New York City. With the arrival of the first waves of immigrants from Eastern Europe in the 1890s, however, this began to change. The Menorah Club movement originated at Harvard College in 1906 with Jewish undergraduates who wanted an opportunity to meet for social and cultural expression. When the Hunter College chapter was established in 1914, the *Wisterion* yearbook described it as a society "organized for the purpose of studying Hebraic culture." The Menorah Club attracted only a small portion of the student body at City College. The movement faded from prominence after World War II, replaced on campuses by the more comprehensive B'nai Brith Hillel Foundation movement, which originated at the University of Illinois in 1923. Under the direction of rabbis who were assigned to work with each campus chapter, its program of culture and sociability took vigorous root on the municipal campuses. Brooklyn College developed the first Hillel Foundation in the New York metropolitan area in 1939. The City College chapter was established in 1943 and grew rapidly after the war. Today, the colleges of CUNY reflect an even greater diversity of religious traditions, and with these traditions has come the organization of new religious clubs.

Even in the 1930s, students at the municipal colleges participated in extracurricular activities, despite the constraints of daily commuting and often the need to work part time. Student life facilities were severely cramped at this time; nevertheless, New York City was actually expanding the municipal college system in the midst of a major economic depression and was keeping the system tuition free for matriculated students—certainly the greatest student service of all. As the decade progressed, the colleges and the Board of Higher Education took steps to create a program of student services that aimed not only to administer student activities but also to nurture the students' personal development.

In accepting the presidency of Brooklyn College in 1939, Harry Gideonse stipulated that he be able to create the position of dean of students as well as develop an active counseling program. In creating this position, he partially anticipated the recommendations regarding student life made later in the 1944 Strayer Report on municipal colleges. This report addresses not only academics but also the entire college experience of students. Drawing on materials supplied by the colleges and their own observations, the study team characterized the student body and recommended a range of services.

[These students] have had to face the many pressures of metropolitan life. Most of them have been reared in small crowded homes where privacy has been at a premium. . . . Many have had to take long rides on subways to and from school. Few have had their perspective on social problems broadened by travel beyond the New York area. A large majority of the students are also first or second generation Americans . . . [and] must therefore be torn between European and American standards, between the codes and customs of their parents, and those of their own group. The students . . . come largely from lower income groups, so that they have grown up in homes where there has been a continuous and severe financial struggle. Since more than 97 per cent of students live at home, parents usually continue to exercise close supervision over their time, friends, and money. In consequence these students lack many of the important opportunities afforded students in a residential college to acquire social poise and self-responsibility.[5]

The survey team recommended that each campus combine existing student services into one department

Beginning in 1957, Baruch College students had the opportunity to enjoy a new addition to freshman orientation. The popular Dean Emmanuel Saxe influenced alumni to contribute funds for entering freshmen to attend Camp Isabelle Freedman in Falls Village, Connecticut, for a weekend before classes started. Faculty, student leaders, and Department of Student Life staff arranged activities that would serve as an introduction to college life. *(Baruch College Archives)*

and work to expand them. In 1946, in conjunction with Strayer Report recommendations, testing and guidance, placement, institutional research, and the supervision of student organizations became part of this department under the direction of the dean of students and chairman of the Department of Student Life.

In just under a century, the municipal college system had gone from maintaining an aloof attitude toward student life outside the classroom to the development of bureaucracies to manage the educational, psychological, and physical life of the student population. Beginning in the early 1970s, each college developed a governance charter in harmony with board bylaws, which included a structure for student life. The CUNY colleges have organized their student services in various ways. Some services were formed on the basis of obvious need, including veterans' services after World War II and the Korean War, and, more recently, child care. A more diverse student body has required a broader spectrum of services. These needs

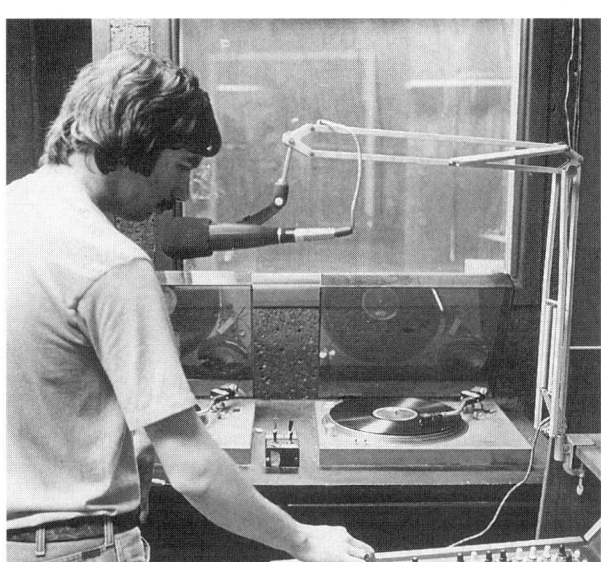

Student-run radio stations offer students valuable experience and fun. This student is operating WBMB at Baruch College. *(Baruch College Archives)*

continue to be met in part by the completion of new student centers, constructed with the financial support of the CUNY Construction Fund. Unfortunately, retrenchments necessitated by the New York City budget crisis of 1976 mean that some CUNY campuses have been unable to maintain the level of personal and career counseling that developed in the decades following the Strayer Report. Since the imposition of tuition in 1976, the financial aid office has become one of the most vital student services.

In 1955, the president of Brooklyn College noted that at least one-third of the college's students had to earn most or all of their living expenses and some contributed to family support; another third had part-time employment. He added, however, that despite this workload, over one-third of the students participated in the more than 300 chartered programs at the college. Today, an increasing number of students enter the institutions as adults with families of their own, which affects these students in new ways. The club hours remain an important opportunity for social participation. The words of President Gideonese, himself an immigrant, spoken in 1955, retain their significance for all CUNY colleges today: "Brooklyn College is deeply committed to the idea that a significant part of the education of its students, who are overwhelmingly children from immigrant homes, must be derived from participation in the varied cultural and social activities of the College as a community in itself and as an agency in the larger community."[6] His experiences are relevant to the situation of current CUNY students, many of them recent immigrants, and his ambitions for them still resonate.

Notes

1. Colie, "The Literary Societies of the College," in Mosenthal and Horne, *The City College*, 481.
2. Canby, *Alma Mater*, 23–25. Also see Horowitz, *College Life*.
3. Watson, *The Brooklyn College Student*, 114.
4. Professor Eva Puder as quoted in Frommer, *City Tech*, 18.
5. New York (State Legislature). . . . *Report of a Survey of the Colleges*. George D. Strayer, Director. II, 9–11. Hereafter cited as *Strayer Report*.
6. Coulton, *A City College in Action*, xii.

5 Student Publications and Journalism

The CUNY student publications of today developed from nineteenth-century prototypes. Although the presidents of City College and the Normal College did not allow student editors to publish materials that were highly critical of their administrations, the students of the 1800s pioneered the yearbooks, literary magazines, and newspapers that today appear on every campus of the City University of New York.

Collegiate newspapers and literary magazines in the United States have always provided an arena for campus leadership. By the 1850s, the students at the Free Academy were ready to produce their own literary magazines. Theodore Tilton of the class of 1854, one of the founders of the Phrenocosmia literary society, recalled over fifty years later that its literary magazine was a "spasmodic publication." "Our little sheet bristled with a crispy secularity—a breezy worldliness especially adapted to 'well-ordered minds.' . . . It irradiated Murray Hill and Lexington Avenue with Baconian wisdom in the form of college jokes, and with vivacious comments on passing events—all set forth with an adolescent freshness of style. . . ."[1] The next publication to appear at 23rd Street was the *Free Academy Microcosm*, created in 1858 under the leadership of future Civil War hero Henry Tremaine (class of 1860). Its first issue aimed to present "a complete record of all the organized societies of the Free Academy" and was published in the form of a broadside sheet divided into four pages. From its beginning, the *Microcosm* conveyed the pride that students felt in the young school.

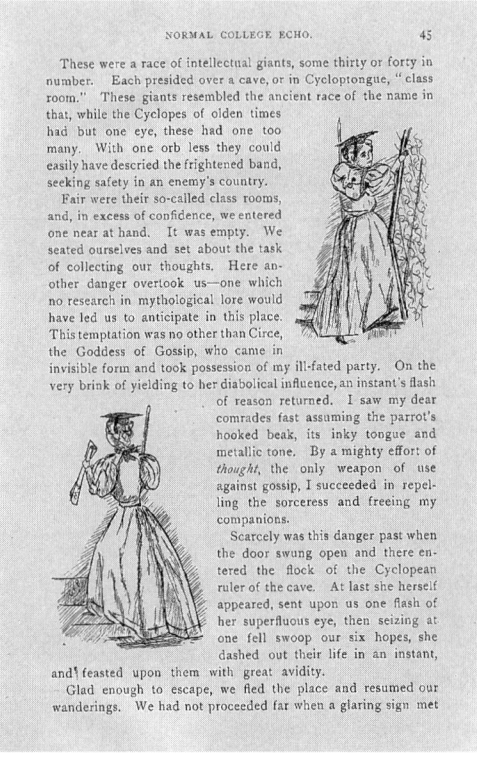

The *Echo* began a proud tradition of student publications at Hunter College. Starting as a vehicle to publish the efforts of two literary societies at the college, it evolved into a publication that gave students the opportunity to express their opinions. The *Echo* later became the *Wisterion*, which remains the name of the yearbook of Hunter College to this day. *(Hunter College Archives)*

This periodical is intended to be just what its name denotes—the little world of the Free Academy. Within its columns will be found all the interesting or important information relative to this institution. . . . [It] may show some of the more venerable, and we might say aristocratic colleges of this country, that the New York Free Academy, although young, and the property of the people is not bind [sic] its old collegiate sisters in any respect.[2]

When the institution changed its name in 1866, the yearbook proudly renamed itself the *Microcosm of the College of the City of New York* and with a few interruptions has provided a yearly record of class activities ever since. The nineteenth century college yearbook was a distinctly American phenomenon, expounding the joys of belonging to fraternities or local secret societies. In 1897, as the nineteenth century drew to a close, women at Hunter College initiated their yearbook, the *Wisterion*. It, too, included information on club activities, religious societies, athletics, and other activities important to the women at the college.

With the opening of new campuses and the development of new programs in the early decades of the twentieth century, additional yearbooks came on the scene. In 1926, the evening session at City College published a yearbook of its own. Although it was not continued, the *Bulletin* conveyed the life and struggles of the evening session students more vividly than any number of statistical reports. The Queens Center of City College issued a quarterly newspaper, the *Queen Bee*, and published a single yearbook, the *Queens Quair*, in 1931. Both were produced with faculty involvement and encouragement and revealed the close relationships that had developed between students and faculty in this small outpost of the large college system. The *Quair* included the center's own song

This issue of *Mercury* typifies the lively graphics that characterized its cover art. Starting as a mixture of news, literary contributions, and humor, "Merc" was devoted to humor after 1914. Like many of the early periodicals, it was begun by students in an association who raised money for the first issues, and for many years alumni editors retained the right to choose the student editors. *Mercury* reflected its times in both content and style. From 1880 to 1900, its tone was somewhat restrained by the sternness of President Webb. The issues of the early twentieth century, on the other hand, reflected the more relaxed atmosphere under President Finley. But *Mercury* really came into its own in the decades after World War I, when the "college man" evolved as a national type. Ben Shahn, who was a student at City from 1920 to 1921, created a cover and sketches of his professors for *Mercury*. A frequent target of *Mercury*'s humor in this period was the Hunter "girl," portrayed as less than the City College male deserved, but at the same time more than he could handle. *Mercury*'s verbal and visual humor was broad, frequently what might be considered "smutty." Strong criticism of professors, economic anxiety, and fear of having to fight in a future war were prominent in its pages. The entry of the United States into World War II saw the suspension of *Mercury*; a somewhat subdued version returned to campus from 1946 to 1958. *(City College Archives)*

College publications provided American women with an opportunity to gain experience not only in gathering and writing news but also in developing skills in finance and publicity. The first page of this May 1914 issue of the newly renamed *Hunter College Bulletin* notes an impending celebration of the change in name from the Normal College, as well as news about matters of interest to many students—the appreciation of literature and women's attempt to obtain the vote. (Hunter College Archives)

and photographs of its newspaper and drama clubs. Students at the City College School of Business started their own yearbook, *Lexicon*, in 1935 as part of their campaign to foster a strong identity for "23rd Street." The first senior class at Brooklyn College initiated the yearbook *Broeklundia* in 1933. The Queens College *Silhouette* began with the graduation of the first class in 1941 and reflected the close relationships that characterized the college's pioneer days. This sense is also conveyed in the yearbooks of community colleges, such as Queensborough's *Aurora*, begun in 1962, and Kingsborough's *Odyssey*, begun in 1966. Their classical titles suggest the respect for learning and the striving for the future so characteristic of CUNY students. The stark title of the New York City Technical College's yearbook, *Statement*, exemplifies a different approach. Almost every unit of the City University of New York has developed a yearbook.

One nineteenth-century publication at City College was short-lived but influential. When the Free Academy became the College of the City of New York in 1866, Richard Rogers Bowker of the class of 1869 started a college magazine, the *Collegian*. Bowker wished to rival the publications of Harvard, Yale, and Hamilton Colleges in literary quality and appearance and thus set out to publish by subscription. His editorial in the first issue included a "mission statement" that could be valid today. "It aims to be always the organ and representative of our students and alumni, and, as such, it will strive always and everywhere to advance the interests of this College, and the general cause of higher education."[3] In each issue Bowker devoted a substantial article to ideas on how to improve the college, reported news from City College and other colleges, and welcomed contributions. Despite the publication's high quality, however, he could not get the number of advertisements needed to keep the price low enough to attract subscribers; the fifteen cent cost seemed too high to many students. The *Collegian* folded after eight issues. In later years, Bowker founded *Library Journal* and *Publishers Weekly*, which are still in existence today.

The 1870s saw the appearance of several journals devoted to the facetious humor of the period; *College Flea*, *Festive Flea*, *Fire-Fly*, and *Mosquito* were representative titles. Most of these publications were the inspiration of a single class and did not survive the graduation of their editors. One of City College's longest-lasting publications, the *College Mercury*, made its debut in 1880, and by the turn of the century it had won a nationwide reputation among college humor magazines. *Mercury* began as a mixture of news and humor, with class notes and some illustrations. Its debut coincided with the rapid development of the elevated railroads, or els, which brought Third and Second Avenue stations to 23rd Street and inaugurated the identity of City College as "Subway University." At first the fare to ride the els was ten cents, considered a hardship by many students, but in 1880 the fare was reduced to five cents for students. A joyous student poet used the April 1880 issue of the *Mercury* to exclaim:

> *O happy student, who can be*
> > *In happiness compared to thee,*
> *The only mortal who can dare*
> > *To ride the El for a five cent fare!*
> *Long did thy noble, suff'ring soul*
> > *Contend ere it could gain its goal;*
> *Long did thy pocket book so bare*
> > *Submit to pay a ten cent fare.*[4]

Mercury disappeared with the coming of World War II, but it returned sporadically in the 1950s and 1960s. Nevertheless, its artwork and outspokenness set a standard for college humor magazines.

City College's newspaper of record was the *Campus*, the first edition of which appeared on September 30, 1907, as a "weekly journal of news and comment." President John Finley saluted it on the first page: "May this new paper help to make and keep our campus on the heights of New York the brightest, cleanest, wholesomest spot in all the city and the place of best friendship and happiest memories."[5] The serious journalism that characterized the *Campus* made it a training ground for many successful journalists, including several who enjoyed long careers at *The New York Times*. Among them were A. H. Raskin ('30), for many years the labor reporter; Fred Hechinger ('43), education editor; Abraham M. Rosenthal ('49), managing editor and then senior columnist; and Michael Oreskes ('75), Washington bureau chief.

Women attending classes at Hunter College were also eager to express their opinions and develop their creativity by establishing student publications. During the early years of the college, the Philomathean and Alpha Beta Gamma literary societies provided an outlet for Normal College women interested in cultivating their literary interests. In 1889 the two societies united and began publication of the *Echo*, a new student magazine. The pages of the *Echo* described European trips and country vacations as well as college festivals and reunions, topics that reflected the interests of the white, Protestant, and middle-class students. However, the publication also actively expressed the opinions of students on serious issues, such as the reorganization of the college curriculum into the Teachers Course and the Classical Course. The editors made it clear to contributors that they were interested in all college affairs. Although they were loyal to the school, they did not hesitate to express opinions critical of some administrative actions.

Many other publications also provided Hunter College students with opportunities for literary expression. In 1911, the Student Council initiated the *Bulletin*. Adelaide E. Hahn, the literary editor, and other

The old and the new mingle on the cover of the first issue of *The City College Accountant*. After the college occupied its new campus on St. Nicholas Heights, the Free Academy Building became the site of a late afternoon and evening commerce course, as part of the new Division of Vocational Subjects. When the faculty of the School of Business and Civic Administration was formally created in 1921, the study of accountancy was a foundation of the curriculum. This publication was succeeded by *Accounting Forum*. *(Baruch College Archives)*

officers of the paper used its pages as a way to focus student opinion. On October 8, 1913, a weekly paper, the *Normal College Bulletin*, became a new organ of student opinion, attesting to the increased interest in student affairs. In 1914, the paper was renamed the *Hunter College Bulletin*, reflecting the institution's new status. It was published under this title until 1948, when it became the *Arrow*. In 1966, the name was changed once again, this time to the *Envoy*.

Soon after settling into the new "skyscraper" that replaced the old Free Academy Building on 23rd Street in 1929, students at City College School of Business showed their determination to establish a distinctive identity for their unit. Initially, *The Campus* covered the news for both St. Nicholas Heights and 23rd Street, but in April 1932 the editor of *The Campus* wrote an editorial that offended the dean of the School of Business, who barred the paper from the building. This dispute might have been resolved, but the next month, on Charter Day, May 7, the *Ticker* appeared, which was produced by School of Business students with faculty support. It immediately replaced *The Campus* as the official newspaper at 23rd Street.

The early years of Brooklyn College strongly reflected the fact that it had originated from a combination of the programs and faculties of the separate City College and Hunter Centers in Brooklyn. The classes, libraries, and laboratories were segregated by sex, as were those at the centers, and the *Pioneer* and the *Spotlight*, the men's and women's newspapers, continued publication until February 1936, when the *Vanguard*, a joint venture, replaced them. This paper had a stormy history, and some felt it favored a "leftist" agenda at the expense of providing a variety of points of view. The Brooklyn College Faculty-Student Committee on Publications withdrew its charter in October 1950, and the *Kingsman* took its place. The rich and flourishing life

Student Publications and Journalism **75**

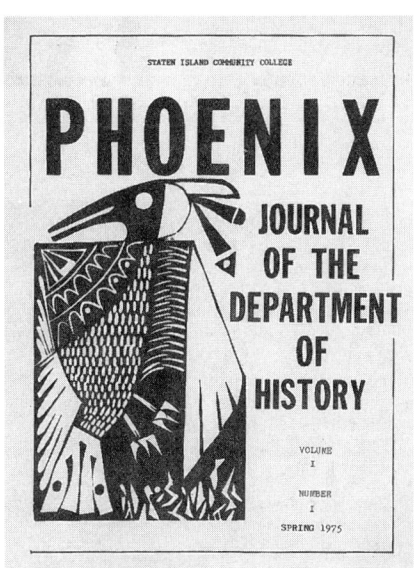

Journals produced by departmental majors are an important part of the CUNY publications tradition. One of the oldest and most prestigious was the *Baskerville Chemical Journal*, named for City College's renowned and inspiring Professor Charles Baskerville. While departmental majors at the four-year colleges have been the most active in creating such publications, the community colleges, with their strong commitment to liberal arts education as well as technical training, have encouraged their students to explore writing in a more scholarly format. *Phoenix*, which was sponsored by the Department of History at Staten Island Community College, reflects its strong liberal arts emphasis. *(College of Staten Island)*

of the School of General Studies at Brooklyn was reflected in its newspaper, *Ken*, launched in 1947. This publication, later succeeded by *Night Call*, joined City College's *Main Events* (founded in 1929) in providing the evening student's perspective on college. In its second decade, Queens College developed the ongoing newspaper *Rampart*, which was followed by the *Phoenix* in 1959. The first name suggested the influence of the veterans who were crowding onto the campus after World War II, whereas the second suggested that a new paper had risen from the demise of the first. As new campuses opened, newspapers quickly appeared to serve as outlets for student opinions. Community colleges as well as the newer four-year institutions all followed suit, with editors creating newspapers to inform students and comment on college affairs.

The rich journal publishing traditions of City and Hunter Colleges were passed on to the School of Business. Baruch's *Accounting Forum* began its long life in 1929. After the school obtained college status, the more wide-ranging *Dollars and Sense: The Baruch College Business Review* appeared in 1979. The expansion of the curriculum at Baruch was also reflected in the appearance of *Encounters: Sentence and Stanzas*, a literary journal inaugurated in 1992.

Most CUNY campuses have at one time published literary journals, their longevity dependent on the recruitment of staff to carry on from year to year. From the 1950s, students in the City College Department of English have published *Promethean*, and aspiring English majors at other colleges have followed this example. *Landscapes* was the literary magazine of Brooklyn College. *Hear Our Voices: The Literary Magazine of Medgar Evers College* (1995) conveys

From 1942 to 1948, *Pulse Quarterly: The Intercollegiate Literary Art Magazine*, staffed by students from Brooklyn, City, Hunter, and Queens Colleges, showcased some of the best student work produced on those campuses. It was printed on heavy stock with colored covers and garnered advertisements for book clubs, concert series, and the like. Its fiction often portrayed the gritty, even grubby, conditions of its students' lives, while the poetry frequently reflected the conflict between students' circumstances and their aspirations. *(City College Archives)*

For over a century the city colleges have been involved in their wider communities. John Jay College has administered a creative writing program for the New York City Department of Corrections for nearly two decades. *The Pen* contains some of the best writing and artwork by students participating in the Inmate Education Program. For many inmates this program provides their first opportunity to express both the realities of their lives and their aspirations for the future. *(Rendering of John Jay College of Criminal Justice by Gary Zaragovitch. Courtesy of John Jay College)*

While best known for its cooperative education business-related programs, LaGuardia Community College has a strong commitment to making the humanities part of every student's education. Music courses, including introductions to jazz and Latin music, and courses in Chinese and Hebrew supplement traditional offerings. The college has a strong "writing-across-the-curriculum" program, in which essays and papers form parts of the required course work in most subjects. Student publications reflect the talents that students bring to the campus, enriched by their work in the humanities and the social sciences. The first student newspaper, imaginatively named *Fiorello's Flute*, was founded soon after the college opened in 1971, and it was succeeded in the early 1980s by the *Bridge*. Student-produced literary journals have included *Harvest*; *Babel*, a quarterly magazine produced by students of foreign languages; and *Indigo*, a literary publication. Others include the *Humanist* and, in the early years, *Genesis*, whose mission statement expressed the drive behind generations of student literary publications: "[There is] no purpose to this magazine beyond that of gaining insight into our own lives and adding meaning to our existence." *(LaGuardia Community College Archives)*

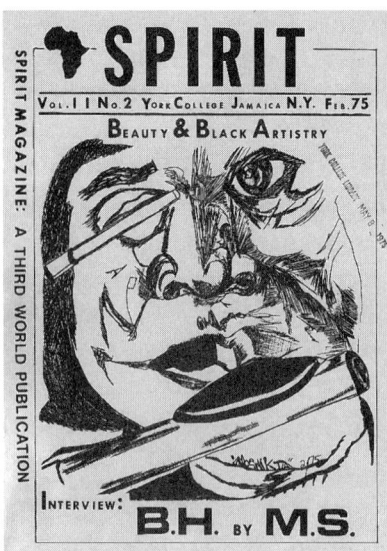

Journals of creative writing, always a popular type of student publication, have continued to flourish at CUNY during the past twenty years. *(York College Archives)*

its own eloquent message, while *The Pen: A Journal of Poetry, Essays and Art*, published by the Office of Special Programs and the Inmate Education Program at John Jay College from 1987 to 1997, reveals not only a play on words but one more aspect of CUNY's history of outreach.

Journals issued by special interest clubs, religious associations, and social groups number in the hundreds, and have provided students with the opportunity to develop not only their writing talents, but also their abilities to organize, meet deadlines, keep records, and publicize their efforts. These publications have ranged from the slick paper and professional quality graphics of the City College School of Engineering's *Vector* to special interest publications laboriously produced on mimeograph machines. Today, desktop publishing allows almost limitless opportunities for good design and ease of production.

Notes

1. Theodore Tilton to Charles F. Horne, ALS, 16 February 1907. Theodore Tilton Collection, City College Archives.
2. *New York Free Academy Microcosm*, No. 1 (January 1858), 1.
3. *The Collegian*, I (November 21, 1866), 1.
4. *College Mercury*, I (April 1880), 1.
5. *The Campus*, I (September 30, 1907), 1.

6 A Call to Action: City University at War

Driven by idealism and a sense of duty, the men—and later the women—of City University have answered the call of the nation. Only eleven years after admitting its first class, the Free Academy saw alumni volunteer for military service as the North fought to preserve the Union and ultimately to end slavery in the United States. As the sparks of conflict ignited the conflagration of the American Civil War in 1861, 30 of the young Free Academy's 200 alumni entered into military service, and a number of the older enrolled students took leaves of absence and enlisted. Many of these students had completed civil engineering courses, which were part of their course of study, and those who remained in school received instruction in military engineering.

Students of the Free Academy formed themselves into an unofficial military company known as the "Free Academy Zouaves" for the sole purpose of defending New York City against possible invasion by the Confederate army. This ardent group of students drilled on the grounds south of the academy on East 23rd Street with equipment and uniforms they bought themselves. Small in number but large in spirit, the members of this unit who were old enough enlisted in local regiments and were sent into battle.

Of the initial enlistees, several Free Academy graduates distinguished themselves on the battlefield. One of them, alumnus Gilbert Hunt McKibbin, class of 1853, saw action in several battles and has provided us

During his Civil War service, Gilbert Hunt McKibbin maintained a regular correspondence with his classmate Alfred G. Compton, then a young instructor at the Free Academy. After returning to civilian life, McKibbin became a textbook publisher and was one of the founders of the New York Athletic Club. He died in 1920. *(City College Archives)*

with a soldier's insight into one of the major battles of the war. In a revealing letter to his classmate and friend Alfred G. Compton, a Free Academy instructor, written in December 1862, McKibbin tells of his unit's plans a few days before the Battle of Fredericksburg: "[T]omorrow at daybreak we are going across the Rappahonock [sic] into Fredericksburg in the face of Myriads of batteries. If we succeed we will have the greatest victory the Union army have yet seen. . . . We are going to have a desperate battle, there will be many head[s] broken and many souls sent hurriedly aloft."[1] This battle proved to be a disaster for the Union army, but McKibbin survived. His courage and leadership

Henry Edwin Tremain, class of 1860, was another Free Academy graduate who distinguished himself during the Civil War. He was promoted to brigadier general and received the Congressional Medal of Honor. After the war, he continued his illustrious career by serving as an assistant U.S. attorney in New York and as editor of *The Daily Law Journal*. He died in 1910. *(City College Archives)*

were evident throughout the war, and he rose to the rank of brevet brigadier general by the time he was mustered out of the army in 1865.

In 1873, the academy (by then known as City College) erected a memorial to its sons who died for the Union. On that occasion, Brigadier General and Medal of Honor winner Henry Tremain, class of 1860, noted that not only had the Free Academy students and alumni provided noble service in time of war, but that the nation could ensure "its own peace, prosperity, and happiness" if the educational advantages its students enjoyed were available nationwide.[2]

In the late 1890s, the nation called upon its youth to serve in another war. Cuban discontent with Spain's rule led Spanish authorities in 1895 to drive large numbers of Cubans from the countryside into concentration camps. Fueled by sympathy for these rebels and driven by Cuba's strategic value to the United States—plus the greed of American business—the United States declared war on Cuba and launched an invasion after the battleship *Maine* exploded in Havana Harbor in February 1898. While the jingoistic "yellow press" led by William Randolph Hearst and Joseph Pulitzer clamored for war, the editors of the City College *Mercury* initially questioned the wisdom of declaring war. Once war began, however, the students supported the invasion, and the faculty voted to grant diplomas to all seniors who enlisted before graduation day. The student support was evidenced by the maps of Cuba and Puerto Rico posted in the halls of the college so that students could track the movement of the American troops.

Prominent among City College men during the Spanish-American War was Aurelius E. Mestre, class of 1881. Mestre was a Cuban émigré who had returned to Cuba to oversee his family's sugar plantation after receiving his degree. When war was declared, Mestre volunteered his language skills and knowledge of Cuba at the service of General Joseph Wheeler, commander of the American volunteers. Mestre's role was substantial by any measure. He assisted in negotiating

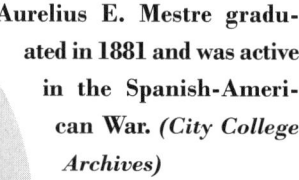

Aurelius E. Mestre graduated in 1881 and was active in the Spanish-American War. *(City College Archives)*

the surrender of Santiago and in arranging the exchange of several U.S. Army officers. On seeing the emancipation of Cuba from Spanish rule in 1899, he remarked that he considered his war service the double duty of one who was both an American citizen and a native of Cuba.

Even though some members of the student body held pacifist sentiments, when the United States entered World War I in April 1917 the men of City College once again responded enthusiastically.

The passage of the National Defense Act in 1916 made all able-bodied male citizens between the ages of

By the fall of 1918 the St. Nicholas Heights campus of City College had been transformed into a military arena. The student concourse in the main building became a mess hall, while the gymnasium served as military headquarters for the nearly 2,000 men in uniform assigned to the college for training of various kinds. The Great Hall, as shown here, was used as a barracks for the Student Army Training Corps, which was made up of all able-bodied students too young for service. The college also supervised activities at an armory on 150th Street and Amsterdam Avenue. The college's president, Sidney Mezes, was a member of the delegation that accompanied President Wilson to Versailles in 1919. He supervised the commission charged with creating the new boundaries within postwar Europe that would recognize Wilson's principle of self-determination of peoples. *(City College Archives)*

Several faculty members made scientific and technical contributions to the war effort. One of the best known was the gas mask, developed by two City College chemistry professors and first used in World War I. Pictured here is a later model of the gas mask used by troops during World War II. *(Brooklyn College Archives)*

eighteen and forty-five members of the Militia of the United States, and thus liable to be called up for military service once the United States declared war on Germany. A City College ROTC unit, authorized in March 1916, drew 500 students in its first month, but it would become the focus of much dissension after ROTC was made compulsory.

In December 1916, the faculty recommended a new elective course, "Theoretical Military Instruction." The months following April 1917 saw the college mobilize fully for "The Great War" with new technical and vocational courses, and the first summer school was inaugurated to help students accelerate their degrees. The first U.S. Signal Corps School in the nation was established at the college, and professors from the chemistry department developed a gas mask, which became standard issue for U.S. troops.

As faculty, graduates, and students of City College were sent to fight in Europe, the women of Hunter College helped in myriad ways. Their fund-raising activities to aid the Red Cross were extraordinarily successful. Their unceasing effort in five Liberty Bond drives raised more than $900,000 for war materials and resulted in the outfitting of four Red Cross ambulances, which were shipped to the war front. Other activities of the Hunter Red Cross Auxiliary led to the preparation of 48,747 surgical dressings needed on the battlefield, as well as the production of 299 sewn garments and 2,493 knitted ones rushed to the troops in combat.

World War I influenced not only those students who fought and returned but also those who entered college in the succeeding decades. In its wake emerged a more worldly student who questioned certain aspects of life in New York City. In earlier generations, student clashes with faculty and administrators, which were not uncommon, reflected a youthful rebellion against authority and lacked any strong political moti-

A Call to Action 83

Hunter College student and alumnae volunteers devoted countless hours to the preparation of thousands of surgical dressings for the medical services. They also sewed and knitted a prodigious number of garments for the U.S. troops in Europe. *(Hunter College Archives)*

The participation of women in America's war efforts dates to the Revolutionary War. However, it was not until the Civil War that women formed Soldiers' Aid Societies and organized themselves on the local level to raise money and supplies for the soldiers. During World War I, Hunter women became part of this tradition of benevolence. Their fund-raising efforts, including Liberty Loan Drives, helped to generate hundreds of thousands of dollars for equipment and supplies. In 1918, this ambulance, named in honor of one of Hunter's noted alumnae, Helen Gray Cone, was one of the four the college sent to the front to aid in the war effort. *(Hunter College Archives)*

vation or agenda. However, the tensions that emerged following the war had a more substantive moral and ethical basis. This was evident by the 1920s, when some City College students led a movement against compulsory military drill—a heritage from World War I—and the presence of an ROTC unit on campus.

By the early 1930s, a growing awareness of international affairs and the worsening economic depression led many students to adopt an isolationist position to the threat of war in Western Europe. For others, cognizance of the horrors of modern warfare as revealed by World War I resulted in an idealistic antiwar position. By 1935, the Popular Front Movement, although dominated by communists, brought together various groups of peace and economic justice activists in a movement to combat fascism in Europe and support social action at home. These political and social themes played themselves out dramatically at City and Brooklyn Colleges, and students at these campuses became leaders in the National Student League and its successor, the American Student Union.

As early as the spring of 1934, students on the campuses of the three municipal colleges joined forces against U.S. involvement in the affairs of other nations. Student newspapers and handbills urged students to boycott classes held between 11:00 A.M. and noon and join in a peaceful protest on campus. The first "Student Strike Against War" was successful and spawned others in the following years, which by then had garnered the support of college administrators. By 1938, the term "rally" replaced the word "strike" to reflect the more accommodating stance of the colleges. The tides of European fascist aggression washed away the student peace movement in the late 1930s, but it was a strong force on municipal college campuses early in the decade. The Hunter College Peace Council, a student organization, was very active until a new president arrived in 1935 who refused to let a rep-

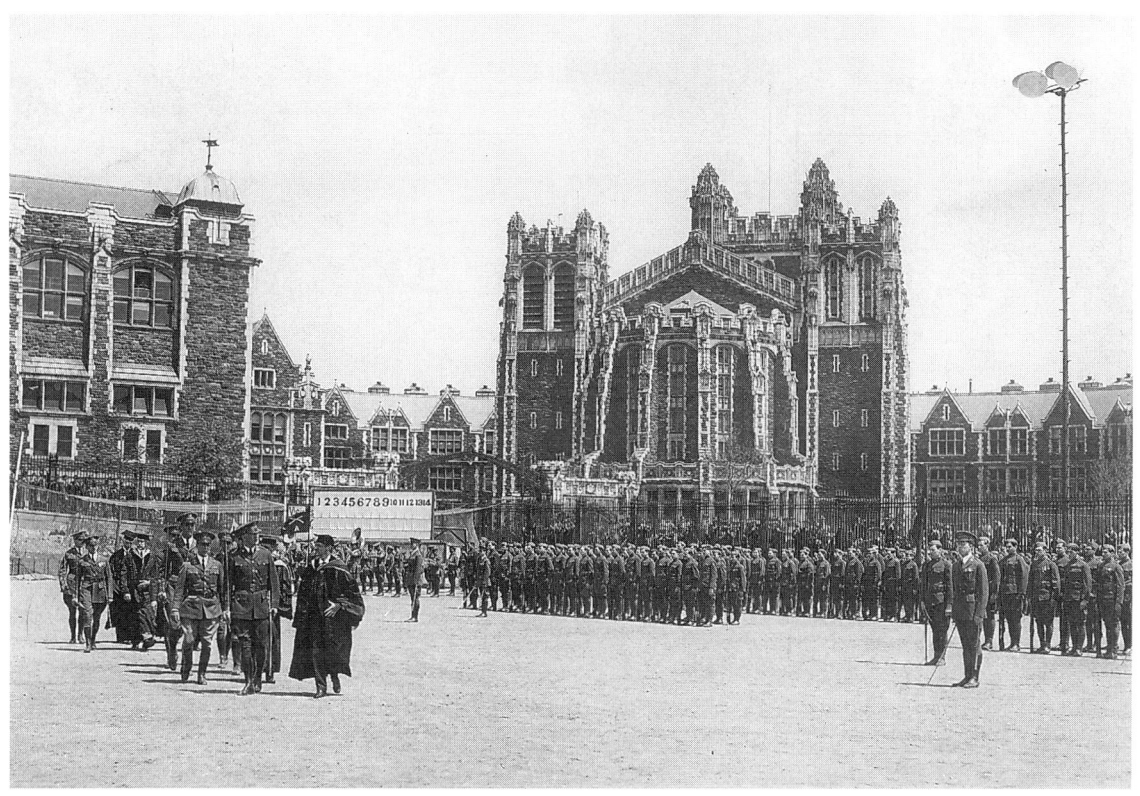

President Frederick B. Robinson reviews the ROTC unit on Jasper Oval in September 1928. When the United States entered the "Great War" in 1917, the City College student body was one of the first to pledge support for the effort by adopting a "resolution of loyalty." The military drills that were instituted in early 1917 became a compulsory part of the college program after the war, until student activism of the later 1920s eventually led to making them an option within the general physical training program. Nonetheless, the college's ROTC unit prospered, becoming one of the largest in the nation. President Robinson, a supporter of the drills, loved the ROTC reviews and always attended them wearing full academic regalia. *(City College Archives/Corbis Images)*

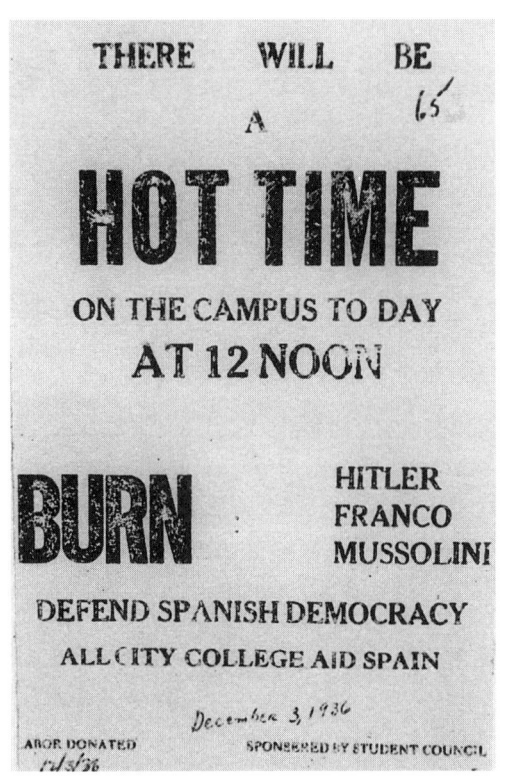

The early 1930s saw a dramatic change in the temperament and mode of student activism. At City College, President Robinson clashed several times with antiwar and antifascist demonstrators. Compulsory attendance at a military review and a college reception for a delegation of Italian students who were personal emissaries of Mussolini caused student unrest. The Spanish civil war (1936–1939) posed a conflict for many students between their wish to see the United States remain aloof from conflicts in Europe and the moral imperative to resist fascism. *(City College Archives)*

resentative of the Women's League for Peace and Freedom address the council and shortly thereafter abolished it. In the midst of the national debate over America's status in world affairs arose a new concern—the Spanish civil war.

The Spanish civil war deeply influenced students nationally, including those at the municipal colleges. Often called the dress rehearsal for World War II, this civil war drew the support of more than 60,000 foreign volunteers who made up the International Brigade that fought on the side of Spain's elected republican government. The ranks of the Abraham Lincoln Battalion of the International Brigade were filled with American volunteers. Drawn primarily from the faculties and student bodies of American colleges and universities, the battalion included dozens of volunteers from all three of New York City's municipal colleges. This contingent numbered approximately 2,800 men. The eventual triumph of the nationalist forces of Francisco Franco in 1939 led students who had not already done so to reexamine their pacifist and antiwar views.

The political ferment of the 1930s was also reflected in some campus publications, particularly at City and Brooklyn Colleges. Each had a Social Problems Club, which functioned as a discussion group and mirrored student concerns with economic conditions and the possibility of another world war. Both their speakers and their publications often generated controversy. City College's *Frontiers*, published in the early 1930s, opposed military training and discussed militaristic developments abroad, as well as the authoritarian policies of some of the college's own administrators. At City College, the activist student press played such an important role that it influenced the "retirement"—actually the resignation—of President Frederick B. Robinson.

Students fearful of being drawn into another world war held their sixth annual antiwar demonstration behind Roosevelt Hall at Brooklyn College on April 20, 1939. The most successful of these rallies, the 1939 rally drew more than 4,000 students under the call for "Peace and the Democratic Way of Life." Unlike the previous rallies, which were dubbed "strikes" and unsanctioned by the college administration, the 1939 rally received the college's support and was referred to as a "peace rally."
(Brooklyn College Archives)

An uneasy interlude followed the end of the Spanish civil war before American forces became totally immersed in the world conflict in 1941. Just months before the attack on Pearl Harbor, a poll taken of graduating seniors of Brooklyn College's evening session showed that most students still opposed U.S. entry into the conflict but believed the country would enter the war by the end of the year. The poll certainly proved prophetic.

Faced with the specter of war, the municipal campuses swelled with patriotism. The Japanese attack on the U.S. naval installation at Pearl Harbor in Hawaii on December 7, 1941, solidified these stirring emotions. The call to duty resounded from all sectors of the municipal college system. The president of Brooklyn College, Harry Gideonse, addressed thousands of students assembled on the campus quadrangle and called for restraint and acceptance: "Patriotism is not a matter of emotion, leaflets, or mass meetings. Rather it is [the] living out of national ideals and values."[3] This message spread across the campuses, and they immediately mobilized. Responding to a federal report citing the need for trained personnel for the war effort, the colleges expanded their programs in the sciences, mathematics, economics, foreign languages, and other related areas. The existing curricula were bolstered and redirected to satisfy the emerging production, administrative, and crucial military needs. By the spring of

World War II saw the full participation of the municipal colleges on the home front as well as through the students and alumni who flocked to the military services. The colleges developed numerous war-related courses such as cryptography, meteorology, the chemistry of explosives, ballistics, navigation, and radio. These students in Dr. Jack Wolfe's class in cryptanalysis are learning one of the many coding systems, known as the "Caesar cipher system." In this system, one or more keywords, such as "Jimmy Doolittle," are put before the regular alphabet for the purpose of mixing them up. Dr. Wolfe shows how it is done with the two rows of letters on the board. The key word could be changed repeatedly to protect the encryption. *(Brooklyn College Archives)*

1942, the municipal colleges had begun to offer the new programs and courses needed for the war effort.

In an arrangement with the armed services, the City College School of Business set up its own Department of Military Science, which offered specialized courses for those entering the armed forces. Hunter added a special "war" course and nursing program. Brooklyn College instituted war-related courses such as cryptography, the chemistry of explosives, meteorology, ballistics, navigation, and radio technology. Male students were required to take additional physical education courses, and all students had to pass a swimming test to receive their degrees. In addition, the college constructed an "American Ranger Course" on its athletic field, comparable to the standards of those at army/navy training centers.

City College responded to the national emergency by providing classes in engineering, mathematics, English, and foreign languages to soldiers chosen for the Army Specialized Training Program. The first ASTP group arrived in April 1943. To accommodate this program, the college transformed the Hebrew Orphan Asylum on the west side of Amsterdam Avenue into a barracks. In January 1943, the Bronx campus of Hunter became a U.S. Navy training station for Women Accepted for Voluntary Service, and thousands of WAVES were housed and trained there. This campus was to respond to one more emergency situation before resuming its educational mission. During the United Nations' search for a hospitable location to house the organization, then Bronx president James Lyons suggested the Hunter site. On March 25, 1946, the United Nations Security Council held its first meeting in the gymnasium building, and the organization remained there for a time before moving to its permanent quarters.

As the war progressed, the number of men and women enlisting in the various services increased.

A year after the United States entered World War II, the Bronx borough president offered the facilities of the Hunter Bronx Center to the U.S. Navy in response to its search for training facilities in the metropolitan area. Training began in January 1943, and on February 9, 1943, *The New York Times* reported the commanding admiral's remarks praising the campus. He felt that no other campus in the area was "so ideally suited as the Hunter Bronx unit to the purpose of preliminary training of WAVES and SPARS." *(Lehman College Archives)*

This is sheet music for the WAVES victory song, with music and lyrics by Muriel L. Schnell of the Brooklyn College class of 1937. Music major Schnell enlisted in the WAVES in January 1943 and immediately applied her talent to composing this song while attending the U.S. Naval Training School in Cedar Rapids, Iowa. In a letter to a friend at Brooklyn, she described her stay at the training school as "a promisingly wonderful experience." In another letter to a former music professor, she related how she used a melody she had composed in her Music 12 class in 1937, noting that "fate found a way of saving [the melody] for this crucial time in our history." The song, arranged for a three-part women's chorus, was adopted by several units of the WAVES and used in numerous battalion rallies and assemblies. *(Brooklyn College Archives)*

According to the records of the Brooklyn College War Counseling Office, by February 1943 more than 2,300 students either had taken an academic leave or had graduated and enlisted. By 1945, the number of Brooklyn College students or graduates who were serving in the war exceeded 7,000. At City College, records indicate the enlistment of over 12,500 alumni, faculty, and students, more than 300 of whom lost their lives for their country.

Even as they were sent to all parts of the globe, many students remained in touch with their former professors and college friends back on campus. At Brooklyn College, Chief Librarian Asa Don Dickinson and other faculty members maintained an active correspondence with many former students, who reported on topics ranging from boot camp training to their combat experiences in all the theaters of war. Former student Lt. Joseph S. Chimento wrote to Professor Dickinson of his Army Air Force training in a letter dated August 16, 1942: "I received my 'wings' as pilot and commission as second lieutenant in the Army Air Force . . . since then I have been on active duty with the 96th Bombardment Squadron and have been assigned to one of the largest class of ships in the Air Force, 'the Flying Fortress.'"[4] The "Flying Fortress" was the U.S. B-17 bomber used extensively in Europe during World War II. The aircraft was so named because of its speed and equipment: thirteen .50-caliber machine guns and a payload of 6,000 pounds of bombs.

From Trucial Oman, Arabia, Corporal Burton M. Blume reflected on the curriculum at Brooklyn with his former economics teacher, Professor Findlay MacKenzie:

> Dr. Kenon has written to me that Mr. Jacobson of the Education Department is a Lieutenant with the AFI in Cairo. No doubt he has been grading some of the

On grounds behind the Midwood campus of Brooklyn College, students prepare for a summer of farming in several upstate New York communities. About a hundred Brooklyn College students spent the summer of 1942 working on farms in the Hudson River region to alleviate the farm labor shortage caused by the war. The students planted, picked fruits and vegetables, packed, graded, and even pitched hay, as well as attended classes two or three evenings a week. This project proved to be a huge success and continued during the summers of 1943 and 1944; it was also extended to farming communities in central New York. Adopting several slogans, such as "Feed a Fighter in Forty-Three" and "Earn and Learn," the project was studied by the government as a way to address the chronic farm labor shortage in the United States. However, with the end of World War II, the project was disbanded. *(Brooklyn College Archives)*

As a member of the Army Specialized Training Program, then Private Bob Dole spent five months on the Brooklyn College campus when he was enrolled in special courses taught by college faculty for the U.S. Army. Brooklyn's facilities were transformed to accommodate the 400 men assigned to this training program. The gymnasium became the barracks, and the college cafeteria served as the military mess hall. Shortly after completing their training, these ASTP soldiers were shipped to all theaters of war. Senator Dole's unit took part in the Italian campaign, and he was severely wounded in an engagement outside of Bologna, Italy, five months after his arrival. During his 1996 presidential campaign, Senator Dole visited the Brooklyn College campus. *(Brooklyn College Archives)*

papers I've sent him. That BC touch is unmistakable. Sort of surprised the theory courses are lagging. What's the matter with this younger collegiate generation? I always sort of favored them. Perhaps, it's a result of the war—functionalism and all that.[5]

As the war concluded, first in Europe and then in the Pacific, legions of veterans returned home to begin or resume their college careers. With the passage of the G.I. Bill in 1943, veterans received support from the federal government for their college studies. This legislation brought a predictable surge in enrollment in all schools and the need for additional student services. At Hunter, a special two-year session for male veterans began on the Bronx campus in 1946. Until 1951 when Hunter in the Bronx became coed, those who completed the program transferred to another

college. City College inaugurated the largest veterans' counseling program in the nation, serving this broad community as well as enrolled students. At Brooklyn College, the War Counseling Office was renamed the Veterans and War Counseling Office in September 1946, and it was redirected to meet the needs of and ease the transition to civilian life for returning veterans. The School of Business at City College addressed the needs of veterans and the wider community by offering an Intensive Business Training Institute of non-credit-bearing courses in advertizing, finance, foreign trade, small-business management, and salesmanship. This immensely successful program continued until 1955.

Unfortunately, as great strides were being made in meeting the educational needs of the veterans, the country faced yet another military conflict barely five years after the end of World War II. On June 25, 1950, North Korean troops attacked South Korea. The United States and other countries responded by sending in troops under the auspices of the United Nations, and fighting continued well into 1953. The effects of the Korean War on young men were profound.

The Selective Service Act was extended indefinitely, affecting all men between the ages of eighteen and a half and twenty-six. Some students enlisted eagerly, but most took advantage of the provision in the law allowing students to complete college and perform service after graduation. At Brooklyn College, where upwards of 2,700 World War II veterans became eligible for service, the Veterans and War Counseling Office was again renamed, this time as the Veterans and Selective Service Counseling Office. Charged with advising veterans on their eligibility for the draft, the office also offered assistance in defining the rights of students. The other municipal colleges had compara-

Since its inception in 1948, the New York Institute of Applied Arts and Sciences had a strong affiliation with the military. This was heightened with the outbreak of the Korean War in 1950, when hundreds of dental lab technicians for the U.S. Air Force received their training at the school. While enrolled, airmen of the 3310th School Squadron were quartered in the St. George Hotel in Brooklyn Heights, just west of the school's Pearl Street location. In addition to providing this technical training, the college served as the site for the New York National Guard Preparatory School for the United States Military Academy. *(New York City Technical College Archives)*

On October 19, 1967, the day that became known as "Black Friday" at Brooklyn College, thousands of students protested against the presence of two navy recruiters on campus. Police were called in to control the mounting number of protesters, and the resulting confrontation led to the arrest or injury of scores of students. Here students outside of Boylan Hall look on during the melee. *(Brooklyn College Archives)*

ble units, which assisted students in filing certificates for deferment or postponement of induction and served as liaisons to local draft boards.

Although World War II veterans and younger students supported the Korean conflict, other students did not widely favor U.S. involvement in the war, and resistance to the draft mounted. Student demonstrations against the war took place on all the municipal campuses. The student presses and student organizations strongly supported this antiwar sentiment; nevertheless, these demonstrations failed to generate broader support. When the Korean conflict ended in an armistice in 1953, the campuses welcomed back a new generation of veterans and proceeded to provide them with educational opportunities and benefits. Politically, the campuses remained quiet for the rest of the decade, despite concerns over McCarthyism and protests against administrative bans on communist speakers. In little more than a decade, however, this situation would change once more.

The civil rights movement of the early 1960s brought increased calls for social and economic justice, and many young people acted on their idealism through marches, sit-ins, and voter registration drives. Student activists allied themselves with a radicalism that questioned all authority, including that of college administrators, who were seen as agents of the "power structure," and they demanded a role in college decision-making. The growing U.S. involvement in Southeast Asia, particularly in Vietnam, intersected with the political and social ferment of the period and sparked protests on hundreds of college campuses. Students were striking out against America's military presence around the world, as well as the threat that it posed to them through the Selective Service laws. This was evident at Brooklyn College, which experienced a student riot in 1967. *The New York Times* headlines of October 19, 1967, read, "Brooklyn Students Battle in Peace

Protest . . . 40 Arrested on Campus." The melee erupted over the presence of two navy recruiters who had been invited to campus, resulting in the "pushing, dragging, punching, club-swinging clash between students and police . . . at its peak, about 1,000 students and 200 policemen were involved in the battle."⁶ Similar incidents were repeated on campuses all over City University and the United States, and were the hallmark of this era of political turmoil and student unrest.

The shooting of students at Kent State University in Ohio and Jackson State University in Mississippi in the spring of 1970 effectively ended the era of major campus protest against the situation in Vietnam. As the war dragged on until 1975, one casualty at CUNY was the closing of campus ROTC units. The lengthy engagement in Vietnam caused many young people to take a less than heroic view of the military. That mindset along with the introduction of an all-volunteer military force removed any strong motivation to enroll in

Jane Fonda, one of the antiwar icons of the Vietnam War era, addresses students on the South Campus of City College. The old Finley Student Center is in the background. *(City College Archives)*

The posters and images on the walls of this Brooklyn College student organization in this 1969 photograph reflect the many social, political, and cultural concerns of students at the end of this turbulent decade. *(Brooklyn College Archives)*

ROTC. Given this backdrop, it is ironic that in the late 1980s General Colin Powell, City College class of 1958, became chairman of the Joint Chiefs of Staff and architect of the successful allied action in the 1991 Gulf War. Dubbed "Desert Storm," this war was fought with the help of numerous CUNY student reservists.

Notes

1. Gilbert H. McKibbin to Alfred G. Compton, ALS December 10, 1862. Theodore Tilton Collection, City College Archives.
2. Henry Edwin Tremain Civil War Dedication, 1873.
3. "Gideonse Speech: Warns Against Hysteria," *The New York Times* (December 9, 1941), as cited in Horowitz, *Brooklyn College*, 114.
4. Joseph S. Chimento to Asa Don Dickinson, ALS August 16, 1942. BC-Student War Correspondence—World War II, Brooklyn College Archives.
5. Burton M. Blume to Professor Findlay MacKenzie, ALS April 10, 1945. BC—Student War Correspondence—World War II, Brooklyn College Archives.
6. "Brooklyn Students Battle in Peace Protest . . . 40 Arrested on Campus," *The New York Times* (October 19, 1967), as cited in Horowitz, *Brooklyn College*, 141.

7 Athletics

In the mid-nineteenth century, college athletics was in its infancy. The role of the Free Academy was to educate the mind, and little attention was given to strengthening the body through participation in competitive sports. Thus, when the school's building was completed and received its first class in 1849, no provision had been made for any sports or exercise facilities. The young men of this class improvised and set about to initiate their own sports program. For them, the area of Gramercy Park surrounding the academy building provided open space for a variety of athletic activities. In addition, the East River, just a few blocks away, served as a perfect venue for swimming and boating sports.

These early students were as resourceful as they were determined to build an athletic program. Even though they lacked the facilities and the support of the school, the students formed clubs and associations and purchased equipment and team uniforms. The first of these clubs included the Reliance Baseball Club, the Free Academy Cricket Club, and a Rifle Association, plus two boating clubs. The boating clubs—the Sophomore Water Witches and the Viking Boat Club—were established in 1861 and were among the first collegiate rowing clubs in New York City.[1] By the time the academy's name changed to the College of the City of New York in 1866, it had both baseball and rowing teams. That same year the student leaders, including Richard R. Bowker, chose lavender and black as the official school colors.

At City College, baseball was the first competitive sport played on the intercollegiate level, and a strong interclass baseball rivalry developed.

In late 1866, the school newspaper, *The Collegian*, reported on the last game of the season between the senior and junior classes:

A fine game was played between the nines of these two classes on Friday afternoon, Nov. 23d, on the grounds corner of 114th Street and First Avenue. The day was quite unpleasant, yet quite a number of '67 and '68 men were on hand. . . . Game was called at 2pm with the seniors at bat. The afternoon was so cold that it was impossible to keep any minute account of the game. The game was closely contested throughout. It was called on account of darkness on the last inning, with juniors at bat and none out.[2]

However, the pinnacle of the 1866 season was City College's 45 to 8 victory over Columbia, played on the Union ballgrounds of Morrisania in the Bronx. This victory brought intense pride to the college and established the "college nines" as one of the top college clubs at that time.

A few years later, in 1872, City College founded its first football club and played under the team motto

With just enough players to cover all the positions, the City College baseball team amassed a record of five wins and one loss against such opponents as Union College, Montclair College, and St. Francis Xavier College during the 1899 season. *(City College Archives)*

"We kick to conquer." The early years of the sport differed significantly from today's version of the game. It was played as an "open" game, where signals, formations, and set plays were limited or nonexistent. The players, outfitted with sweaters, short pants, and stockings, lacked the protective equipment used today.

Needless to say, injuries among the players were numerous. The team played informally until 1876, when growing interest in the sport led to the introduction of intercollegiate games. Teams originally played on a lot at 130th Street and Sixth Avenue and later moved to Central Park. Football was played sporadically over the years at City, generating fierce rivalries with other schools in the system, particularly with Brooklyn College in the late 1930s. However, the football teams fielded were generally weak, and both City and Brooklyn dropped the sport in the 1950s.

Lacrosse is the longest continuously played sport at the college. As with other sports, it began informally, with the first lacrosse team organized in 1887. By 1895, lacrosse had evolved into a highly competitive sport.[3] Over the next two years the City team won both the United States Championship and the Dominion Championship in Canada, and in 1903 it captured the National Collegiate Lacrosse Championship.

The Normal College, like the Free Academy, slowly added physical education and sports to the daily routine of college life, failing in its early years to recognize the importance of athletics to the total development of women. The permanent home of the Normal College (later Hunter College) on Park Avenue and 68th Street was designed without a gymnasium, and it had only a small calisthenium. But attitudes about the importance of physical education for women began to change in the latter decades of the nineteenth century. Women throughout the country took up the bicycle craze, reflecting a new independent spirit. This height-

By the 1890s, City College students had developed a wide variety of team sports, as indicated by this wood engraving in the 1891 *Microcosm.* **(City College Archives)**

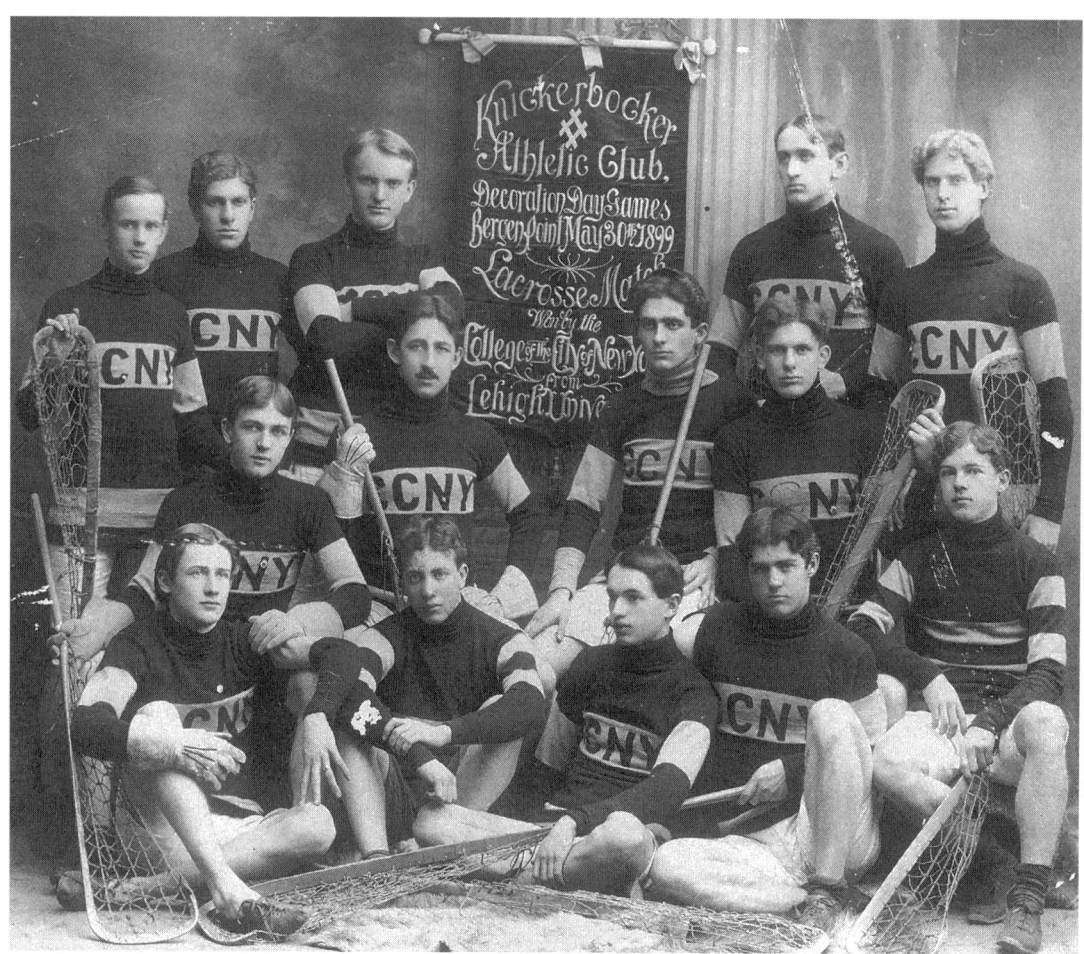

First played at the college in 1887, lacrosse has the distinction of being the longest continuously played sport at City. By the late 1890s the lacrosse team was a formidable, highly competitive team that had won several major intercollegiate championships. The team is shown here with the banner celebrating its win against Lehigh University in a tournament game sponsored by the prestigious Knickerbocker Athletic Club on May 30, 1899. *(City College Archives)*

"We kick to conquer." The early years of the sport differed significantly from today's version of the game. It was played as an "open" game, where signals, formations, and set plays were limited or nonexistent. The players, outfitted with sweaters, short pants, and stockings, lacked the protective equipment used today.

Needless to say, injuries among the players were numerous. The team played informally until 1876, when growing interest in the sport led to the introduction of intercollegiate games. Teams originally played on a lot at 130th Street and Sixth Avenue and later moved to Central Park. Football was played sporadically over the years at City, generating fierce rivalries with other schools in the system, particularly with Brooklyn College in the late 1930s. However, the football teams fielded were generally weak, and both City and Brooklyn dropped the sport in the 1950s.

Lacrosse is the longest continuously played sport at the college. As with other sports, it began informally, with the first lacrosse team organized in 1887. By 1895, lacrosse had evolved into a highly competitive sport.[3] Over the next two years the City team won both the United States Championship and the Dominion Championship in Canada, and in 1903 it captured the National Collegiate Lacrosse Championship.

The Normal College, like the Free Academy, slowly added physical education and sports to the daily routine of college life, failing in its early years to recognize the importance of athletics to the total development of women. The permanent home of the Normal College (later Hunter College) on Park Avenue and 68th Street was designed without a gymnasium, and it had only a small calisthenium. But attitudes about the importance of physical education for women began to change in the latter decades of the nineteenth century. Women throughout the country took up the bicycle craze, reflecting a new independent spirit. This height-

By the 1890s, City College students had developed a wide variety of team sports, as indicated by this wood engraving in the 1891 *Microcosm*. (City College Archives)

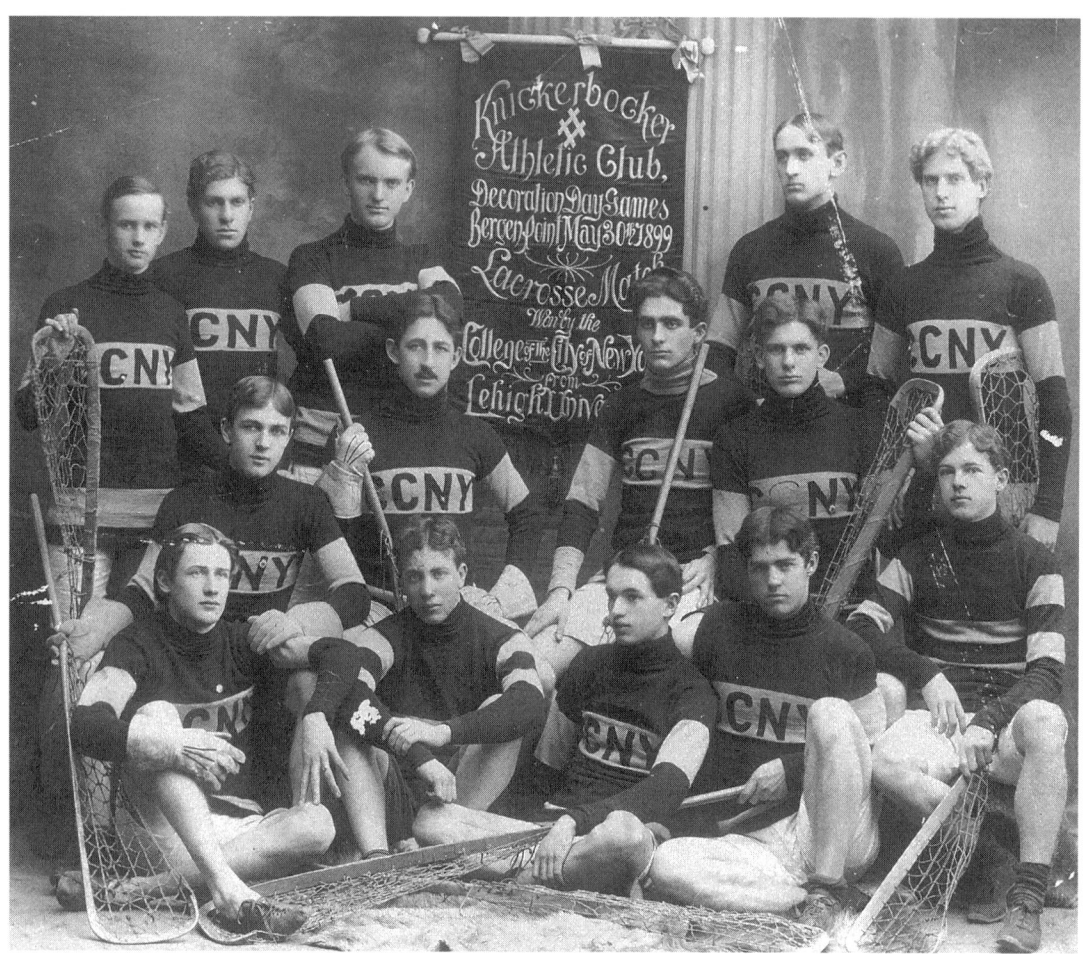

First played at the college in 1887, lacrosse has the distinction of being the longest continuously played sport at City. By the late 1890s the lacrosse team was a formidable, highly competitive team that had won several major intercollegiate championships. The team is shown here with the banner celebrating its win against Lehigh University in a tournament game sponsored by the prestigious Knickerbocker Athletic Club on May 30, 1899. *(City College Archives)*

ened awareness of the benefits of physical activity led to the creation of Normal College bowling, tennis, and basketball teams. By 1900, the basketball team, known as the "Normal Five," traveled to competitions as far away as Staten Island, New Paltz, and Northampton.

Athletics at City College received a tremendous boost from the 1907 move to St. Nicholas Heights. Several new sports were introduced, and students now had a gymnasium and a pool. John Finley, the new president, was a staunch advocate of the classical belief in a sound mind and body, and immediately set out to develop a strong physical education program. He recruited an outstanding athletic director to coordinate the sports teams and direct the physical training program. By the 1920s City College boasted a major athletic program, with membership in key intercollegiate associations and new swimming, water polo, and gymnastics teams. In 1915, the college opened Lewisohn Stadium, which gave students their own athletic field to accommodate football and track.[4]

In 1919, City College recruited and hired Nat Holman, star of the Original New York Celtics, to coach City's basketball team, and under his leadership it became one of the preeminent teams in the country. His coaching career peaked in 1950, when the City College Beavers swept both the National Invitational Tournament and the National Collegiate Athletic Association Championships, an accomplishment un-

Originally known as the Manual Training Team, the "Normal Five" traveled to play basketball at colleges throughout the northeast. The creation of this team marked the college's first attempt to organize sports for its women students.
(Hunter College Archives)

Members of the Brooklyn College boxing team are shown conducting an inter-team sparring round refereed by boxing coach Nat Doscher in 1939. *(Brooklyn College Archives)*

matched to this day. Unfortunately, this sterling moment in the college's basketball history was tarnished a year later with a point-fixing scandal involving several City players. The college was not alone; this type of scandal affected many college basketball teams in the United States, including a Brooklyn College team earlier in 1945.

Like other colleges within the municipal system, Brooklyn College began in 1930 with extremely limited physical education facilities. The first "campus," composed of rented office space in several buildings in the downtown area of Brooklyn, had only an improvised gymnasium space. Like their City and Hunter College predecessors, students at Brooklyn College were resourceful and utilized the athletic facilities that were available within the borough of Brooklyn. The women used the swimming pool at the Pierrepont Hotel, and the football team traveled to the Fort Hamilton High School field in Bay Ridge for practices and games. Years later one player recalled: "The team practiced in various public parks and abandoned lots, and it meant lugging duffel bags bulging with sweaty shoulder and thigh pads on long journeys by subway and trolley car. . . ."[5]

The completion of the Brooklyn College Midwood Campus in 1937 improved the lot of both men and women student athletes by providing a pool, a gymnasium, and an athletic field. Although the training facilities were vastly improved, Brooklyn never fielded consistently strong or successful teams, because the

Athletics   103

City College basketball coach Nat Holman is pictured with his players after winning the National Collegiate Athletic Association Championship in 1950. Holman reached the pinnacle of his coaching career when the City College team performed the unprecedented feat of winning both the National Invitational Tournament and the National Collegiate Athletic Association Championships. Holman had taken the City College basketball program from its home gym and small attendance to the court at Madison Square Garden, where it played before an audience of 18,000. *(City College Archives)*

City College became fully coed in September 1951, and the alumni magazine lost no time in informing its readership about the developing athletic program for women. *(City College Archives)*

Football was first played at City College in 1872. The varsity team, organized in the 1920s, had its greatest success in the mid-1930s under Coach Benny Friedman. Brooklyn College established a varsity team soon after its opening in 1930. Students and faculty gave minimal support to these teams, although they enjoyed greater popularity with alumni. Brooklyn College President Harry Gideonse, a strong supporter of college athletics, remarked: "Nothing is more ironic than to think of football and athletics as a necessity in Minnesota and as a luxury in Brooklyn." But despite his commitment, Brooklyn College football was disbanded in 1954, although it was briefly revived in the 1980s. At City College, football was officially "suspended" in the fall of 1951. *(Brooklyn College Archives)*

college never emphasized athletics over academics. Harry Gideonse, the college's long-time president, expressed this sentiment succinctly: "Members of our teams are students who play, and not players who register."[6]

Soccer was introduced at City College in 1915. However, a lack of qualified players forced the school to drop the sport for several years after its successful first season. Although a team, known as the Lavender Soccer Club, was selected again in 1923, it really was not until after World War II that soccer took hold at City, Brooklyn, and Queens Colleges. With the creation of the Metropolitan Soccer League in 1947, soccer catapulted ahead of other sports teams in the system. At Brooklyn College, the soccer team maintained an outstanding record from 1936 to 1961 under the leadership of its coach Carlton H. Reilly, whose teams won eight league championships, enjoyed six undefeated seasons, and set a winning streak record of twenty-four games. The Brooklyn team gained added prominence when two of its players were named to All-American ranking—George Andreadis in the early 1950s and Helmut Poje in the early 1960s. Soccer's popularity extended to two of the community colleges as well. New York City Community College established soccer as a varsity sport in 1958, followed by Staten Island Community College in the early 1960s.

Tennis was officially instituted at City College in 1911, but it was not regularly played until 1918. For City, the sport's halcyon year was 1942, when its team

Brooklyn College boasts many sports teams for women. The Brooklyn College women's archery team is shown practicing in the Roosevelt Hall Gymnasium in 1966. *(Brooklyn College Archives)*

Coach Joseph Smith, a National Fencing Hall of Fame member, guided the Brooklyn College fencing teams from 1930 to 1963. During this time, the women's team won five national intercollegiate championships. *(Brooklyn College Archives)*

Under the leadership of Coach John Dolan, the Staten Island Community College soccer team posted a winning record for several seasons in the 1960s. *(College of Staten Island)*

won ten straight matches to capture the New York City championship. Brooklyn College, too, secured a prominent role in intercollegiate tennis with the play of Eileen Rahlens from 1959 to 1962. She led the Brooklyn team to its first undefeated season and won two consecutive Eastern Collegiate Tennis Championship titles.

City College established swimming as a competitive sport in 1906, but as with other sports, it took several years before it was completely organized. The 1912–13 season was perhaps City's first complete season, when the college beat the more established teams of Cornell and Columbia Universities. City College recorded its first Metropolitan Championship in 1939 with a record of seven wins and one loss. Both Baruch and Brooklyn Colleges offered their students the opportunity to compete in this sport as well. Carol Frick, a noted diver, was the first Brooklyn College student to compete in the Olympics, and she helped the Brooklyn team secure the Eastern Intercollegiate Championship for three straight seasons.

Although most schools within the system supported track and field teams, track first became a varsity sport at New York City Community College in 1947. Between 1947 and 1956, the team posted an impressive record by winning the Mile Event in the Penn Relays for four consecutive years.[7]

By 1952, Queens College supported twelve intercollegiate teams, three of which were for women. As with the other schools, the first priority of the Queens sports program was the development of individual character, with team victory second in impor-

Women's athletics at City College first flourished at its School of Business (now Baruch College), where a number of team sports were played, some at the varsity level. *(Baruch College Archives)*

tance. Teams competed in the major sports of baseball, basketball, and soccer and had excellent coaching staffs. The strong varsity program was based on an equally strong intramural program, which afforded every student an opportunity to compete in a sport. As players progressed, they could opt to play for one of the varsity teams, which entered into intercollegiate play.[8]

The intramural team concept, as employed at Queens College, was a huge success throughout the municipal college system. At Brooklyn College, intramural sports began in the late 1930s, and in each succeeding year interest grew. By the early 1950s, 60 percent of men played in the intramural tournaments, and by 1957, more than 50 percent of the entire student body, both men and women, participated. During the early 1960s, the Brooklyn College program expanded from four to twelve sports, drawing thousands of spectators to games and matches.

In the 1970s, intramural sports attracted more women to competitive sports than ever before. This period witnessed an increase in women's varsity sports teams. Women gained athletic opportunities not only in basketball and some of the other more traditional women's team sports, but also in sports new to women, such as track, volleyball, softball, and gymnastics. With the growth of intramural play, the CUNY system created an increased opportunity for intercampus play.

In 1986, the CUNY Athletic Conference was formed to promote the "highest standards of competition, interests, integrity, and efficiency in the administration of intercollegiate athletics." Currently, the four- and two-year colleges have their own divisions within the conference, with four-year colleges competing at the Division III level of the National Collegiate Athletic Association.

The lack of formal athletic fields did not deter these Baruch College runners in the 1970s. However, with new facilities scheduled for completion on many CUNY campuses early in the new millennium, athletic facilities will rival those of many urban colleges. *(Baruch College Archives)*

Hunter College is shown enjoying its victory in basketball at the CUNY Sports Conference playoff in 1997. *(Photo provided by Photography Services of the Consolidated Edison Company of New York, Inc.)*

Notes

1. Taft, "One-Hundred and Fifty Years of Sports," *City College Alumnus* 68 (7 June 1973), 9.
2. *The Collegian* 1 (December 5, 1866), 6
3. Taft, "One-Hundred and Fifty Years of Sports," *City College Alumnus* 68 (7 June 1973), 14.
4. Dunlap, "Games of Champions," *Alumnus* 92 (Summer 1997), 12.
5. Horowitz, *Brooklyn College*, 16.
6. Ibid., 99.
7. Frommer, *City Tech*, 16.
8. "Intercollegiate Teams Rapidly Making Progress in Developing Talent Through Inter-Murals," *The Queens Page* (January 1952), 13.

8 Access and Excellence: 1960–1997

In the midst of World War II, the New York State Legislature appointed a committee to survey the municipal colleges of New York City. Named to head the committee was George D. Strayer, professor emeritus at Columbia University's Teachers College and an experienced evaluator of academic institutions. Its report, issued in the spring of 1944, was both far-reaching and far-seeing. Ranging from an evaluation of the elevator service at the School of Business to the role of graduate work, the Strayer team report emphasized: "The Board of Higher Education is clearly charged with the development of a *system* of higher education for the City of New York." The report recommended that the college presidents and the Board of Higher Education together "establish the broad purposes and the general characteristics of an integrated system of higher education for the City of New York" and consider, among other questions, "what kinds of students and how many students should be educated."[1] Tied to this question were considerations of expanded access, the nature of the educational programs to be offered, the types and cost of graduate education, and the role of adult education programs. The team asked each college to define its mission within the system and for the Board of Higher Education to work with the Board of Education in developing postsecondary programs of one or two years' duration. Noting the inadequate facilities, the report recommended an ambitious construction program, as well as expanded student services, and the infusion of generous amounts of financial assistance from New York State to make all this possible.

At the end of 1960, fifteen years after the cessation of World War II, the municipal system still consisted of the four four-year colleges, along with an expanded community college system brought about by the creation of Staten Island, Bronx, and Queensborough Community Colleges. In general, facilities remained overcrowded. The Strayer report had, for example, recommended an entirely new plant for Queens College. By the end of 1960, the college had erected new science and physical education buildings but still depended on the small buildings of the original Parental School, augmented by unsightly Quonset huts. Because of the inadequacy of the facilities, it was necessary to raise the averages required for admission at both the four- and the two-year colleges. In addition, the increasing populations of African American and Hispanic students in the high schools were underrepresented in the public colleges. Tuition was still free for all students who qualified for matriculated status at the four-year colleges, as had been the case since the first class entered the Free Academy in 1849.

Just before the outbreak of World War I, then City College president John Finley had envisioned a publicly supported university in New York City. In 1936, under the headline "One Big University Proposed for City," *The New York Times* reported that Board of Higher Education and Hunter College officials were recommending the establishment of a "University of

Mina Rees, the first head of the City University Graduate School, is shown in her office on West 42nd Street across from the New York Public Library in 1964. A professor of mathematics and dean at Hunter College, Rees provided the leadership and vision that spurred the development of doctoral programs soon after the municipal and community colleges were federated into a university in 1961. Today its doctoral faculty of more than 300 includes scholars from the colleges and from the Graduate School as well as researchers from major New York City institutions such as the Botanical Gardens, the Museum of Natural History, and the Metropolitan Museum of Art. The Graduate School grants all CUNY doctoral degrees. *(CUNY Central Office Archives)*

the City of New York," which would offer graduate and professional training, coordinate the programs of the municipal colleges, and "meet the growing academic need of a wide area and a vast population expansion."² Queens College was established the next year, but New York City did not act on the larger recommendations. The Board of Higher Education took up the question again in 1960, and at the end of the year its Committee to Look to the Future recommended transforming the system of municipal colleges into a university system authorized to grant the doctoral degree. The following year, on April 11, 1961, Governor Nelson Rockefeller signed into law the bill creating the City University of New York (CUNY). This same bill eliminated the legislative mandate for free tuition and gave the Board of Higher Education the ability to impose charges if it chose to.³

The need for expanded programs and access was great. In 1960 the combined facilities of CUNY permitted it to accept just 13 percent of the city's high school graduates, or 8,563 students. New York City's municipal colleges had become highly selective institutions, unlike the public colleges and universities in other states. In emphasizing the need for increased access, the 1944 Strayer team commented: "A democratic society needs more than just an intellectual elite. . . . A large group of liberally educated persons is not a luxury, but a necessity in a democracy. Students of exceptional ability are not the only ones, therefore, who deserve four years of liberal education."⁴ To help realize this aim, the board's Committee to Look to the Future issued "A Long-Range Plan for the City University of New York, 1961–1975" in September 1962. The report's theme was expansion. It projected a rise in enrollment and urged $400 million in capital expenditures to accommodate that increase. The report further recommended that provision be made to admit the upper 30 percent of New York City high

The first CUNY Ph.D. students to receive their doctorates are shown in this 1965 photograph with Chancellor Bowker and Dean Rees. The following year the Graduate School and University Center occupied redesigned quarters at 33 West 42nd Street, which were noted in the architectural press for their simple elegance. In 1999, the Graduate School moved to the extensively renovated B. Altman Building at 34th Street and Fifth Avenue, where it joined the Oxford University Press and the New York Public Library's Science, Industry and Business Library.
(CUNY Central Office Archives)

school graduates to the four-year colleges and one-third of all high school graduates to the community colleges.

In 1963, Albert H. Bowker left his post as dean of Stanford University's graduate school to accept the chancellorship of CUNY. Bowker wished to develop doctoral programs and centralize policymaking for the university, but he soon saw that his greatest challenge lay in meeting the needs of the projected increase in applicants and taking into account their ethnic diversity. CUNY began to acknowledge and respond to the fact that for many African American and Hispanic high school students in New York City, economic and social adversity was linked to educational deprivation more than it had been for poor immigrant students in the early part of the century. The board's 1962 long-range plan did not sufficiently address this problem, so a new effort began.

The pioneer years of the Borough of Manhattan Community College are reflected in this photograph that shows one of the scattered rental facilities in west midtown that made up its "campus" between 1964 and 1982. In common with the community colleges established in the 1950s, the Borough of Manhattan Community College initially had space and staff to accommodate only a small percentage of the students who could benefit from its programs.

In 1982, the Borough of Manhattan Community College moved to a multipurpose building on Chambers Street in lower Manhattan, and now, with more than 16,000 students, has the largest community college enrollment within CUNY. Its need for more space was recently met by Miles and Shirley Fiterman's gift of an office building on West Broadway. The college's location near the World Trade Center, the financial district, and the artistic communities of SoHo and TriBeCa adds strength to its programs in business administration, data and word processing, corporate and cable communications, and human services. The liberal arts transfer program allows students to earn the A.A. or A.S. degree. The Borough of Manhattan Community College provides an extensive continuing education program to its community and moderately priced dance, theater, and music events through its TriBeCa Performing Arts Center. Special outreach programs include the Family College, Kids College, and the Corporate Training Center. *(CUNY Central Office Archives)*

The period between 1964 and 1972 saw remarkable growth in the CUNY system, when the university expanded through the designation of the branches of City and Hunter as separate four-year colleges, the establishment of four new community colleges, and the creation of three new four-year colleges. In addition to the establishment of the Borough of Manhattan Community College (1963), Kingsborough Community College (1964), Hostos Community College (1969), and LaGuardia Community College (1971), CUNY assumed jurisdiction over New York City Community College in 1964. Tuition was eliminated at all the public two-year colleges in the city, and they began to develop curricula in distinctive technical and business fields while providing a general education or liberal arts major. Embracing the "community" concept of their names, they initiated adult and continuing education programs and General Educational Development (GED) work, in addition to offering exhibits and performing events for the enrichment of their communities.

In 1968, the Bronx center of Hunter College became a separate four-year college, named for Herbert H. Lehman, New York State governor (1933–43) and U.S. senator (1949–57). In 1953, the City College School of Business was renamed for Bernard M. Baruch of the class of 1889, the international financier and advisor to presidents. Concern over the need to improve the quality of the school, in both its business and its professional programs, led the City University to commission a study by Donald E. Cottrell, whose 1950 report on public education in the city had been so influential. His report of 1962, "Education for Business in the City University of New York," recommended severing the school's ties with City College and creating a new college of business and public administration. The Baruch School faculty favored this recommendation. After much discussion and con-

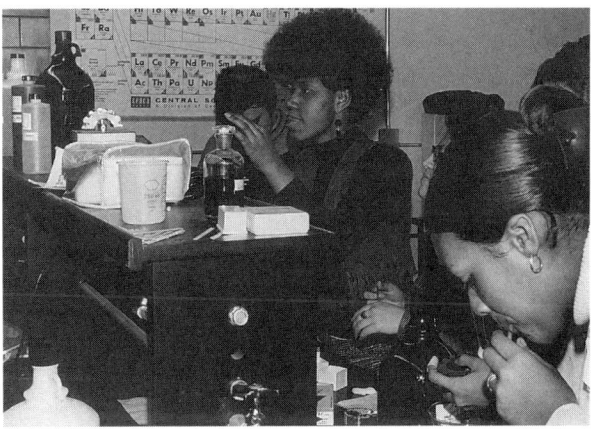

These students are participating in a basic chemistry course at Eugenio Maria Hostos Community College in the 1970s. Hostos, which was named for a nineteenth-century Puerto Rican patriot and educator, began with a mission to serve the people of the South Bronx. Since it welcomed its first class in 1970, Hostos has reached out to Spanish-speaking students who come to New York City from many countries. Its bilingual undergraduate education program allows Spanish-speaking students to begin college level studies while taking the English as a Second Language course sequence, with the aim of continuing and completing their studies in English. Career programs include accounting, dental hygiene and medical laboratory technology, gerontology, and public interest paralegal studies. The program in liberal arts and science includes the traditional academic courses as well as the visual and performing arts and African, Latin American, and Caribbean studies. Its continuing education program, art gallery, and two theaters, housed in the new East Building, enrich its South Bronx community. *(CUNY Central Office Archives)*

Since it opened in September 1971, Fiorello H. LaGuardia Community College in Long Island City has actively involved students in planning their education. Volunteers recruited from the first class are shown in a summer 1971 program to assist students entering in September; participants also developed recommendations for college governance and other areas of student life. LaGuardia was initially established to bring a college program to the residents of western Queens, but its cooperative education programs have attracted students from throughout the city. Through the "co-op" program, all day students undertake two mandatory work experiences as part of their requirements for the associate degree. The college is a leader in the use of microcomputers for instruction—particularly in the teaching of writing and mathematics. Although its emphasis is on career programs, the college encourages its students to look ahead to further education through its bridge and transfer agreements with fifty public and private four-year colleges, including those in CUNY. In its tradition of service to the neighborhood and to the wider city, which is an integral part of the community college mission, LaGuardia maintains an extensive Division of Adult and Continuing Education. This division administers the largest non-federally funded program for deaf adults in the country, as well as an Institute of Sign Language Interpretation. The college also trains emergency medical technicians, paramedics, and bilingual home health aides. The associated campus high schools include the highly regarded Middle College High School, the International High School for recently arrived immigrants of high school age, and the Robert F. Wagner Institute for Arts and Technology. These schools have been models for college and high school collaborations throughout the nation. *(CUNY Central Office Archives)*

John Jay College of Criminal Justice traces its origins to the program in police science created in 1955 with the Baruch School of Business and Public Administration. Since 1964 it has been a four-year liberal arts institution with specialties in criminal justice, public service and fire science, forensic psychology, police science, corrections administration, and security management. It offers several programs leading to the master's degree, as well as the course work for the university's Ph.D. program in criminal justice. Through supervised internships, the college provides its students with practical experience in criminal justice, working at government and private agencies. Other members of the student body work in police and fire departments, or with security and correctional agencies, and pursue bachelor's and master's programs for professional development and personal enrichment. The "campus" consists of two buildings near Columbus Circle; one of these, which formerly housed a city high school, was spectacularly renovated in the 1980s.

Scholarly journals, such as *Fire Science Review* and *Criminal Justice Ethics*, published by various programs within the college, reflect John Jay's distinctive programs. *(Institute of Criminal Justice Ethics, John Jay College)*

sideration of alternative proposals to bring the Baruch School to St. Nicholas Heights or to keep it at 23rd Street, the Board of Higher Education approved a separate four-year college bearing Baruch's name in 1968. City College, meanwhile, added two new schools, for nursing and architecture, in that same year.

One of the three new four-year colleges established at this time, John Jay College of Criminal Justice (1964), grew out of the program in police science developed at the Baruch School in 1955. This program had succeeded the cooperative program established with the New York City Police Department in the 1920s. The other two new colleges, designed for communities that traditionally had little access to higher education, were York College (1966) in Jamaica, Queens, and Medgar Evers College (1971) in the Crown Heights section of Brooklyn. On the opening day of classes at Medgar Evers College, *The New York Times* reported this statement by Dr. James A. Moss, the vice-president of academic affairs: "We're here to challenge the whole notion that a college should be an isolated place outside the life of the community."[5] During its early days, the college was located in eight different sites, including the former Brooklyn Preparatory School and three storefronts near the intersection of Bedford and Nostrand Avenues.

All this activity was focused on expanding opportunity in New York City, but facilities, vital as they were, did not alone address the issue of access that had become increasingly important in the years since Townsend Harris had written, "Open the doors to all." Students studying under the G.I. bill were gone by the early 1950s, but the early 1960s felt the influx of "war babies" and postwar babies, or "baby boomers." Space constraints collided with a larger pool of applicants and drove the required average for admission into the upper 80s, with the possibility of having a cutoff of 90 percent for the four-year colleges by 1964. Such a

York College, created in 1966, reflected the Board of Higher Education's determination to expand access to the City University of New York. Space requirements had influenced admissions policies to the city's public colleges ever since the Free Academy building became overcrowded after the Civil War. In the nineteenth century when City College and the Normal College (Hunter) were required to take students directly from the common schools, they used admissions examinations as a selection device. With the development of public high schools in the 1890s, a high school diploma became the sole requirement for admission. City and Hunter were able to accommodate all high school graduates who applied because in the next few decades only a small minority of the seventeen- and eighteen-year-olds in the city actually graduated from high school. This open admissions policy ended in 1924 when the number of applicants began to exceed the places available. A high school average of 72 percent was then made the cut-off point for admission to matriculated status. When New York raised the age for mandatory high school attendance to sixteen in the 1930s and the number of high school graduates began to increase substantially, the municipal colleges started to turn away many students who could have succeeded in college. By 1940 students needed an 80 percent average to gain matriculated status at City College, and the figure rose steadily in the 1960s.

York College, designated "Alpha College" for Queens in October 1966, and renamed York two years later, was the fifth senior college in the CUNY system. The next year it admitted its first class of 378 students to temporary quarters in Bayside. In 1968, the Board chose Jamaica for a permanent location. York operated in trailers on the campus of Queensborough Community College in Bayside (shown here) and from 1971 to 1986 occupied temporary spaces in Jamaica, where students are shown registering. Since 1986 York has occupied its own fifty-acre campus in Jamaica, dominated by the extensive Academic Core building. The Core houses classrooms, lecture halls, laboratories, art studios, and support services, while nearby are health and physical education facilities, science buildings, the theater, and the auditorium. York offers a broad baccalaureate curriculum with programs in the liberal arts, business, health, and cooperative education and confers B.A. and B.S. degrees in education, nursing, and accounting. Rooted in the Jamaica community, York College maintains a close liaison with many of the social, religious, governmental, and business agencies in Queens. *(CUNY Central Office Archives)*

requirement excluded many qualified students. The kinds of unskilled jobs that had provided adequate living wages for generations of New Yorkers were dwindling. Education beyond high school was becoming a necessity rather than a luxury for young people, not only in terms of personal enrichment but for economic survival. New York City had changed in other ways since the end of World War II as well. While the population remained constant in the 1950s, its makeup had changed. About 700,000 whites left for the suburbs, many lured by low-cost G.I. mortgages. An almost equal number of African Americans from the south and residents from Puerto Rico arrived in the city, supplementing the numbers of such families who had made their homes here for centuries.

To help expand access, the Board of Higher Education issued a revised master plan for CUNY in 1966 that called for the admission of graduates of any high school program (not just the academic course) who were in the top half of their class. The requested funding was not forthcoming, forcing the university to cut back its 1966 freshman class by 2,500 students.

Medgar Evers College, like other CUNY colleges established in the 1950s and 1960s, was housed in a variety of temporary facilities before achieving a permanent campus. The college admitted its first class in the fall of 1971 and was administered from this Crown Heights brownstone for several years. The name of the college honors the civil rights activist Medgar Wiley Evers, who was killed in 1964. It offers both associate and baccalaureate degrees. Programs in its School of Continuing Education address the needs of persons seeking career advancement or specialized training. Closely associated with its Crown Heights/Bedford-Stuyvesant neighborhood in Brooklyn, Medgar Evers offers programs in liberal arts and science, business, education, computer applications, and nursing. The biological and environmental science programs stress research. Support services help the multinational student body to succeed and include basic skills, English as a Second Language, career planning and counseling, and cooperative education.
(CUNY Central Office Archives)

Admission to both community and four-year colleges continued to require high standing in a college-preparatory high school course.

Chancellor Bowker persevered in his efforts to increase the number of minority students in CUNY by outlining a new admissions program in 1968, which guaranteed admission to the top one hundred graduates from each of sixty public high schools. This plan recognized the fact that students in inner city high schools often earned lower averages than students of similar class rank in other high schools, and that they had less access to college-preparatory courses. When the Board of Higher Education passed Bowker's resolution, it noted that CUNY enrolled more African American and Puerto Rican students than any other "integrated institution of higher education in the United States," and that "constructive ethnic integration of the student bodies of the City University [was] itself an essential step toward the creation of an integrated society." It went on:

> [T]he Board finds it of crucial importance to move further and faster in the direction of the historic mission of the public college system of New York City, which has been to provide expanding education opportunities, particularly for those whose backgrounds of social, educational and economic disadvantage identify them as most needful of the special concern and assistance of the City University.[6]

Early the next year the New York State Board of Regents "Statewide Plan for the Expansion and Development of Higher Education" endorsed the Board of Higher Education's resolution to enroll all high school graduates by 1975. High-quality postsecondary education for all young people who wanted it was becoming a social necessity.

In February 1969, a minority coalition, called the Committee of Ten, presented five demands to Buell G. Gallagher, the president of City College. The first three illustrated required adjustments rather than major changes at the college. The core demand was that the student bodies at the college reflect the ethnic makeup of the public high school system of New York City. No specific agreement on points four and five could be reached. The situation worsened in March as Albany announced that it would reduce its contribution to CUNY. The Black and Puerto Rican Student Coalition, an outgrowth of the Committee of Ten, joined with other students to mobilize against the reductions. Although more than 13,000 CUNY students rallied in Albany on March 18, the university still received an appropriation of $29 million less than it had requested.

The Black and Puerto Rican Student Coalition called for a boycott of classes on April 21, which was somewhat effective. Early the next morning about 200 members of the coalition entered the south campus, evicted all others from the buildings, and chained the gates shut. The coalition announced that the newly proclaimed "University of Harlem" would remain shut until the five demands were met. President Gallagher suspended classes, promised not to call in the police, and formed a group to negotiate with the coalition. During this time ad hoc faculty groups met and made many recommendations. After several days a few elected officials from both New York State and New York City instituted court proceedings that resulted in the reopening of the college on May 5. The following days were chaotic in contrast to the discipline that the coalition had maintained. Police entered the campus, and protests and strikes in support of the "Five Demands" appeared on several other CUNY campuses

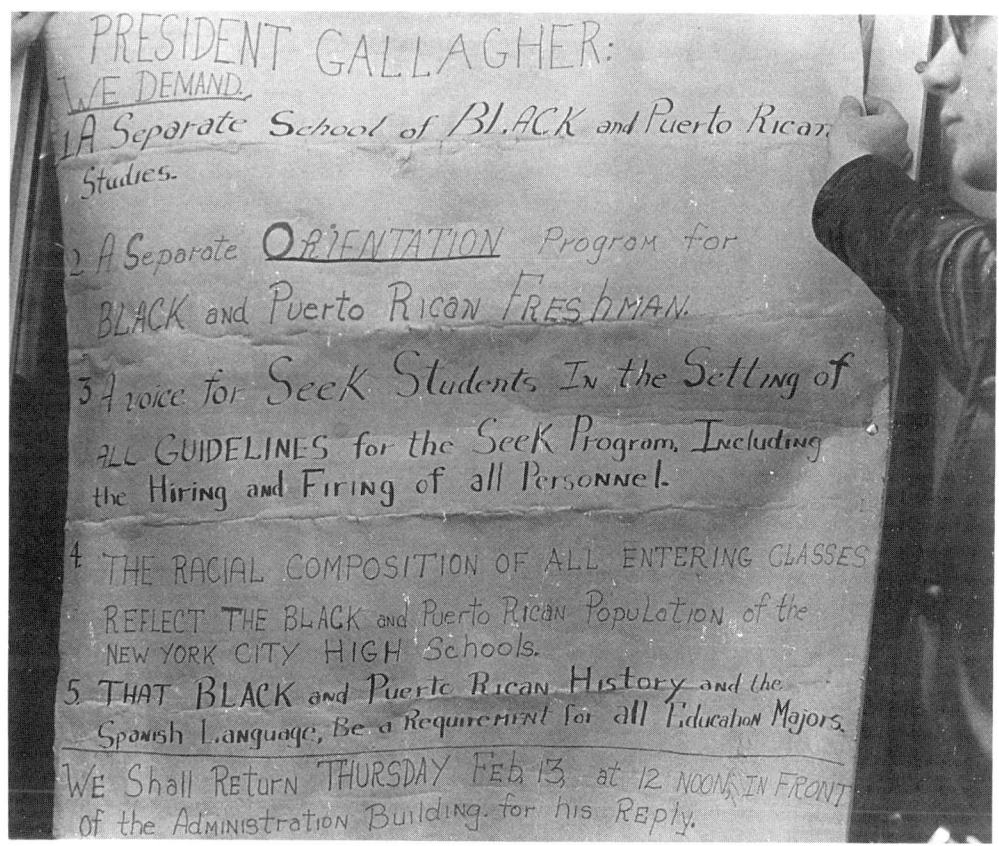

as well. President Gallagher resigned. For many administrators, instructors, and students, the need to offer broader access to the university was no longer an issue—the question had become one of method. On July 9, 1969, the Board of Higher Education passed a resolution accelerating the implementation of the policy of universal access, which had been approved by the Board of Regents for 1975, to the fall of 1970. The policy guaranteed all high school graduates a seat at a CUNY college; however, it did not and does not guarantee admission into the college of choice, or, necessarily, to a senior college. The Board's goal of achieving "ethnic integration of the colleges" has been achieved over the past three decades, as students from various ethnic groups and cultures have enrolled in the university.

From the initial call for a School of Black and Puerto Rican Studies at CUNY has come the development of many departments and programs of African, African-American, Puerto Rican, Caribbean, and Hispanic Studies over the last three decades. Similar programs have emerged at colleges throughout the country. *(City College Archives)*

The pressure of events in late April and early May 1969 began as localized demands for changes at City College, but soon swept the entire university. This led to consultations between the Board of Higher Education and educational and civic groups as to how wider access might be fairly implemented. With the support of the United Federation of Teachers, the Central Labor Council, the Public Education Association, the City College Alumni Association, and the CUNY University Senate, the Board of Higher Education moved its goal of 100 percent admissions from 1975 to September 1970 in a resolution passed at its meeting of July 9, 1969. The plan approved at that meeting specified: "It shall offer admissions to some University program to all high school graduates of the city."[7] The final plan guaranteed students graduating with an average of at least 80 percent, or who were in the top 50 percent of their high school graduating class, a place in a four-year college. All others could attend a community college. Popularly labeled "open admissions," the new policy did guarantee a seat to every high school graduate, but not necessarily at the college of his or her choice.

> Under open admissions, CUNY exhibited the features of a system of universal higher education: like the primary and secondary schools, it was free and publicly supported and it provided a next rung on the educational ladder for those who had advanced beyond the earlier steps. The open-admissions policy attempted to lay to rest the often-debated question about who should be educated. This was the question on which selective admissions policies had been based and which in part had led to differences in the educational attainment of various class and ethnic groups.[8]

In the fall of 1970, almost 35,000 students entered CUNY for the first time—over 24,000 more than had entered in the fall of 1969. Campuses rented additional space and made new use of existing space. The CUNY program went beyond the open enrollment systems of large state universities. Through sequences of remedial courses in mathematics, writing, and study skills, the university actively helped students to succeed in college work. During the early 1970s, the City University received additional funds to accommodate the instructional needs of a much larger student population. Strong remedial and counseling programs were designed to help students gain the necessary skills to succeed in the various degree programs. The state approved the master plans, which would eventually create new, expanded facilities for City and Hunter Colleges. With support from the CUNY Construction Fund and the Dormitory Authority of the State of New York, the four-year colleges made ambitious construction plans. City College's North Academic Center and two new buildings at Hunter were completed in the early 1980s. A total renovation of the Willowbrook hospital site on Staten Island gave the College of Staten Island a new campus in 1987. Almost every campus of CUNY has benefited from construction made possible by the fund. It has transformed CUNY, providing the facilities and equipment necessary for the maintenance of institutional quality.

In early 1972, Governor Nelson Rockefeller recommended that CUNY be absorbed into the State University of New York (SUNY) and adopt its tuition structure for matriculated undergraduates as well as for graduate students and nonmatriculants. While proponents of the governor's scheme maintained that most CUNY students would receive federal and state tuition assistance, which would cover their costs, it could be predicted that any tuition charge was sure to increase. Moreover, assistance plans cover only eight semesters of college, and many of CUNY's new students would need longer to complete their studies. Family and work responsibilities, plus the need for

In 1965, the Board of Higher Education expanded the public educational opportunities available in Staten Island through the creation of Richmond College, an upper division college offering the last two years of work needed to complete the bachelor's degree. Richmond College remained small and in 1976 merged with Staten Island Community College to create the College of Staten Island, the only public college in the borough of Richmond. The College of Staten Island had two campuses until 1994 when they were consolidated through a move to the site of the former Willowbrook Institution. The neo-Georgian buildings are set among 204 acres surrounded by woods and ornamental landscaping and form the largest college campus in New York City. The campus features state-of-the-art infrastructure and computer systems with numerous multimedia laboratories, and its Faculty Center for Excellence in Pedagogy and Media Technology builds on this strength. The college offers nine master's degree programs and an advanced professional certificate in education supervision and administration, as well as collaborative programs with Staten Island high schools for both students and teachers. The Center for Developmental Neuroscience examines the health effects of air and water pollution of the Fresh Kills Land Fill. The astrophysical observatory with its sixteen-foot dome was completed in 1996. With a theater, a concert hall, a recital hall, and an art gallery, the College of Staten Island is a center for cultural life on Staten Island. *(Courtesy of CUNY Office of Facilities Planning)*

The postwar period brought the beginning of aid from the state of New York to the municipal colleges. Legislation passed in 1948 supported teacher education programs, and legislation of 1959 and 1960 bound the state to pay for one-third of the cost of the first two years of undergraduate education for each student in the senior colleges. Greater reliance on state aid made budget decisions in Albany increasingly important to the City University in the 1960s at the same time that Governor Nelson Rockefeller and his supporters were urging CUNY to impose tuition equal to that at the State University of New York. From the mid-1960s until 1976 spring rallies on campuses against the threat of tuition mobilized many students and faculty members. Campus delegations traveled to Albany to meet with legislators to ensure that CUNY received needed funding in the state budget. As shown in this photograph, delegations summarized their views on signs, the most popular of which read "Our position: no tuition" and "Who does Nelson think we are? Rockefeller?" Rockefeller was no longer governor in 1976 when New York City's budget woes reached a crescendo. The Board of Education was forced to use its power to charge tuition in return for state funding of the senior colleges. The community colleges receive the bulk of their public funding from New York City. *(City College Archives)*

noncredit remedial courses, meant that graduation in the traditional four years was unrealistic for many. In the spring of 1976, the financial woes of New York City, compounded by those of New York State, created a crisis. Unable to meet its payroll, the university closed for two weeks at the beginning of June. After intense negotiations, the Board of Higher Education agreed to use its power to impose tuition. In exchange, Albany would take responsibility for funding the four-year colleges, and CUNY would retain its separate status as a university system. In 1979, the Board of Higher Education of the City of New York officially became the Board of Trustees of CUNY, a change that reflected the decreased municipal role and the shared role of the mayor and the governor in appointing board members. Access to the four-year colleges became more restricted, as students were required to be in the upper third of their high school graduating classes rather than the upper half. The university was down, but the creativity and resilience that have characterized it over the decades ensured that it would not be defeated.

Over the past decade, state aid has diminished in relation to costs, and the colleges of CUNY must rely more on tuition and fees, federal and foundation grants, and private donors. In addition to grant-funded research sponsored by the National Science Foundation and the National Aeronautics and Space Administration, the individual colleges have received grants from the National Endowment for the Humanities, the Ford Foundation, the Mellon Foundation, the Fund for the Improvement of Postsecondary Education, the Aaron Diamond Foundation, and a host of others. These grants validate the quality of CUNY programs.

In addition to its doctoral programs in the arts and sciences, the City University has developed well-regarded professional schools. The CUNY Law School at Queens College dates from 1983, while the Graduate School of Library and Information Studies, a Queens College program, was initially established in 1955 as a course of study to train school librarians. The program expanded over the years and in 1971 was fully accredited by the American Library Association as a graduate degree program. Today the school also trains academic and public librarians as well as students focused on such specialties as law, health sciences, and corporate librarianship. Hunter College's School of Social Work also has its roots in the 1950s, having been established in 1958. Its Master's of Social Work program is accredited by the Council on Social Work Education.

The fully accredited Schools of Engineering and of Architecture and Urban Planning at City College also serve the entire CUNY community. Undergraduate and master's degrees are granted by the college, whereas the CUNY graduate school awards doctoral degrees in engineering—civil, mechanical, chemical, electrical, and computer science. The Sophie Davis School of Biomedical Education/CUNY Medical School, also located at City College, encourages applications by minority students underrepresented in medical schools. The medical school is based on the programs of the Sophie Davis School, which, since 1973, has integrated undergraduate education with the first two years of medical school. The seven-year program leads to the Bachelor of Science and Doctor of Medicine degrees. The first five years of the program, which are taken at City College, include the basic science portion of the medical school curriculum. The final two years of clinical training are offered at one of the seven New York State medical schools that cooperate with the program and that confer the M.D. degree. Students in the program are encouraged to provide primary care to underserved communities.

Since 1983 the City University of New York School of Law at Queens College has trained law students to use their skills in the public interest. As a result, nearly half of its graduates take jobs in public interest law, as opposed to the 2 percent nationally who follow this path. To this end, the curriculum includes the study of professional responsibility and roles and alternatives to the adversary system, such as mediation, as well as traditional legal studies. Diversity is a hallmark of the school, as is its strong clinical program, which ranks among the top ten nationally. The school grants the J.D. degree. *(Courtesy of CUNY Office of Facilities Planning)*

The Free Academy was established during an era of heavy immigration to New York City, and as City College expanded to its St. Nicholas Heights campus in 1907, new immigrant groups were arriving from Italy and Eastern Europe in large numbers. The effects of the restrictive and discriminatory Immigration and Nationality Act of 1924 meant that by the end of World War II, many of the white students at the colleges came from families a generation removed from the immigrant struggle. The open admissions era coincided with forces that were bound to affect the applicant pool for CUNY. The restrictive immigration laws were revised in 1965 and again in 1978, and as a result students entering CUNY were very diverse. Prior to 1970, citizenship was required for matriculation, except in exceptional circumstances where the Board granted waivers. From 1970 on, applicants only had to be "bona fide residents of New York City." Once tuition was implemented, this requirement was dropped, as the colleges admitted students who received their secondary schooling abroad.

The admissions changes of 1970 benefited not only African American and Hispanic students but also Asian American and other ethnic populations. Some of these students, as well as those who had been educated abroad, entered CUNY with impressive educational preparation, but needed work to master English. The teaching of English as a Second Language thus became an important part of CUNY's mission. Lillian Kovar, a professor of sociology at Bronx Community College, described the students she taught in the 1990s: "[T]hey represent a seeming multitude of cultures, comprising African American, Puerto Rican, Indian, Colombian, Haitian, Jamaican, Antiguan, Barbadian, Nigerian, Guyanese, Vietnamese, Italian, Jewish, and a host of others, a panorama of the developing world in microcosm."[9] Additional changes at CUNY stemmed from concern over the numbers of students in need of remedial work in reading, writing, or mathematics and the resulting lower graduation rates at some colleges, as well as concern over the reduced funding from New York State. The Board of Trustees has recently put in place more rigorous admission requirements for the four-year colleges, as well as strict conditions concerning any remedial work offered on their campuses. While English as a Second Language programs and departments have been part of the colleges' curricula for many years, the University administration has recently inaugurated its own Language Immersion Program for applicants needing intensive work in English before beginning college work; the "CLIPS" (CUNY Language Immersion Programs) are now being inaugurated on several campuses. In the early 1990s, the university's College Preparatory Initiative urged high schools to offer traditional college-preparatory courses in science, mathematics, and foreign languages and to counsel students on the importance of taking them. These steps make the four-year colleges more rigorous in their admission requirements than the large state university systems and many private colleges.

In the 150 years from 1847 to 1997—from the Free Academy to CUNY—those involved in public higher education in New York City have periodically reexamined the implications of the words that Horace Webster addressed to the first entering class of eager young men and their anxious elders on a January day in 1849:

> The experiment is to be tried, whether the highest education can be given to the masses; whether . . . the children of the whole people can be educated; and whether an institution of learning of the highest grade can be successfully controlled by the popular will, not by the privileged few, but by the privileged many.[10]

His words have a new potency and poignancy today.

Established in 1958, Queensborough Community College's Bayside campus in northern Queens has a suburban atmosphere. The majority of the college's graduates continue on to a four-year college after obtaining associate degrees. The arts degrees include programs in fine art and photography, whereas the career programs feature such cutting-edge studies as laser and fiber optics technology, as well as programs in health sciences, nursing, and engineering-related studies. Special services to the community include the External Education Program for the Homebound, which brings classroom experience to the homebound via the conference telephone, a comprehensive, noncredit continuing education program, a professional performing arts series, and performing and fine arts programs sponsored by the academic departments. *(Courtesy of CUNY Office of Facilities Planning)*

Kingsborough Community College, "CUNY's college by the sea," occupies a spectacular setting on a sixty-seven-acre campus in Manhattan Beach that is bounded by Sheepshead and Jamaica Bays and the Atlantic Ocean. The college, which admitted its first class in 1964, has career programs that include business administration, fashion merchandising, community mental health, and journalism, as well as travel and tourism, nursing, and sports, fitness, and recreation. Half of its 15,000 students pursue such programs while the others work toward the A.A. or A.S. degrees that will enable them to transfer to four-year institutions as juniors. Kingsborough works with the Board of Education in several collaborative programs that include the My Turn program for Senior Citizens and the Family College, which helps parents on public assistance complete their education while their small children benefit from an on-campus satellite school. The widely praised College Now program was initiated in 1984 under the combined sponsorship of the college, the City University of New York, and the New York City Board of Education. It provides high school students with the opportunity to earn up to eight college credits and to improve their mathematics, writing, and reading skills. The U.S. Department of Education has cited this program as a model high school/college partnership. Testing, individualized courses of study, and counseling support high school seniors in the program who may choose courses in the humanities, science, social sciences, mathematics, and English. The program strengthens the skills needed for academic success and has helped hundreds of students to make a smooth and successful transition to college work.

Kingsborough Community College sponsors a year-round series of cultural events, including a Summer Music Festival and a Children's Theme Festival. Shown in this picture is the Marine Academic Center. *(Office of Public Relations, Kingsborough Community College)*

Notes

1. *Strayer Report*, Chapter I, 1–2.
2. "One Big University Proposed for City," *The New York Times* (March 24, 1936).
3. Chapter 398 of New York State Laws of 1961.
4. *Strayer Report*, Chapter II, 17.
5. "Medgar Evers College Opens," *The New York Times* (September 19, 1971).
6. New York (N.Y.) Board of Higher Education, *Minutes of Proceedings* (1 August 1968), 181.
7. New York (N.Y.) Board of Higher Education, "Statement of Policy" in *Minutes of Proceedings* (9 July 1969), 188.
8. Lavin, Alba, and Silberstein, *Right Versus Privilege*, 307.
9. Kovar, *Here to Complete Dr. King's Dream*, 3.
10. Webster, "Address of Horace Webster" in *Addresses Delivered upon the Occasion of the Opening of the Free Academy*, 27.

Afterword

The 150-year history of the City University of New York, which was told in the preceding pages through pictures retained by individual college archives and administrative offices, relates a story that is as much a history of urban politics as a history of a municipal educational institution. From the time that Townsend Harris first proposed the Free Academy in 1846, politicians and educators have debated its funding, admissions, curriculum, educational theory, political loyalties, and facilities. The visibility of the City University of New York makes it vulnerable to scrutiny by all public sectors. This scrutiny has molded the institution, which has always been ready to adapt to meet the new demands of a constantly evolving society.

However, the ultimate measure of the success of an educational institution is its graduates and their contributions. Since the first classes graduated from the Free Academy and the Normal School, thousands of CUNY graduates have entered the teaching profession. Many have entered other professions, such as medicine, law, business, and the sciences. CUNY graduates have made their mark in all fields. Many have received wide public recognition and academic or professional honors; eleven are Nobel laureates. More challenges await the CUNY community in the future, but pride in our past accomplishments should lead us into the new millennium confident that the generations of students to follow will make their own contributions to the city, the state, and the nation.

Bibliography

The authors share responsibility for the text. Barbara Dunlap compiled the bibliography with the assistance of Sandra Roff and wrote the index; Anthony Cucchiara prepared the photographs.

Abel, Steven. "Sic Transit Lewisohn Stadium." *City College Alumnus* 61 (June 1966):7–10.

Addresses Delivered upon the Occasion of the Opening of the Free Academy, January 1849. New York: William C. Bryant & Co., Printers, 1849.

[Alfassi, Itzhak]. "B'nai Brith." In *Encyclopaedia Judaica.* New York: Macmillan Company, 1971.

Annual Report of the President of the Normal College for the Year 1870. New York: The New York Printing Company, 1871.

Beecher, Catherine. *Educational Reminiscences and Suggestions.* New York: J. B. Ford and Co., 1874.

Bender, Thomas. *New York Intellect: A History of Intellectual Life in New York City, From 1750 to the Beginnings of Our Own Time.* New York: Alfred A. Knopf, Inc., 1987.

Berrol, Selma. "A College Is Born [Baruch College]." *Urban Education* 25 (April 1990): 25–36.

———. *Getting Down to Business: Baruch College in the City of New York, 1847–1987.* New York: Greenwood Press, 1989.

Bildersee, Adele. "State Scholarship Students at Hunter College of the City of New York." Ph.D. diss., Columbia University, 1932.

Blumstein Elder, Renée Joy. "An Investigation of the Effects of Student Personality and College Climate on College Outcomes of an Urban Commuter College [City College]." Ph.D. diss., Columbia University, 1986.

Bonelli, Vincent F. "Bronx Community College." *The Bronx County Historical Society Journal* 16 (Fall 1979):51–61.

Bronstein, Arthur J. *Lehman College: The Voice of Youth.* Bronx, New York: Herbert H. Lehman College of the City University of New York, [1970] Herbert H. Lehman Memorial Lecture, 1970.

[Bryden, J. A.]. "Newman Apostolate." In *New Catholic Encyclopedia.* New York: McGraw-Hill Book Company, 1967.

Burchard, Lewis Sayre. "A Chat about Professor Compton by an Old Graduate." *City College Quarterly* 10 (March 1914):5–33.

Burns, Mae A. "An Historical Background and Philosophical Criticism of the Curriculum of Hunter College of the City of New York from 1870 to 1938." Ph.D. diss., Fordham University, 1938.

Cahalane, Cornelius. "Police Training." *Annals of the American Academy of Political Science* 146 (November 1929): 166–69.

Canby, Henry S. *Alma Mater: The Gothic Age of the American College.* New York: Farrar & Rinehart, 1936.

Carman, Harry J. "Address at the Fourth Anniversary of the Dedication of Queens College." *School and Society* 54 (December 27, 1941):601–03.

Chenoweth, Karin. "The New Faces of College [York College]." *Black Issues in Higher Education* 15 (July 9, 1998):26–28.

The City College of New York: Sesquicentennial. New York: The City College of the City University of New York, 1997.

City University of New York. Board of Trustees. *Minutes of Proceedings of the Board of Trustees of the City University of New York.* New York, N.Y.: The Board, 1979–1996.

City University of New York. University Task Force on Student Retention and Academic Performance. *Report of the Uni-*

versity Task Force on Student Retention and Academic Performance. [New York]: City University of New York [1984].

Cohen, Arthur M., and Florence B. Brawer. *The American Community College*. San Francisco: Jossey-Bass, 1982.

Cohen, Robert. *When the Old Left Was Young: Student Radicals and America's First Mass Student Movement, 1929–1941*. New York: Oxford University Press, 1993.

Cosenza, Mario Emilio. *The Establishment of the City College of the City of New York as the Free Academy in 1847 (Townsend Harris, Founder): A Chapter in the History of Education*. New York: Associate Alumni of the College of the City of New York, 1925.

Cottrell, Donald. *Education for Business in the City University of New York*. New York: Chapman, Evans and Delehanty, 1962.

———. *Public Higher Education in the City of New York: Report of the Master Plan Study*. New York: Board of Higher Education of the City of New York, 1950.

Coulton, Thomas Evans. *A City College in Action; Struggle and Achievement at Brooklyn College, 1930–1955*. With a foreword by Harry D. Gideonse. New York: Harper, 1955.

Cremin, Lawrence. *American Common School: An Historic Conception*. New York: Bureau of Publications, Teachers College, Columbia University, 1951.

———. *American Education: The Metropolitan Experience, 1876–1980*. New York: Harper and Row, 1988.

———. *American Education: The National Experience, 1783–1876*. New York: Harper and Row, 1980.

"A Debate on the Future of the Baruch School," *City College Alumnus* 62 (January 1967):12–18.

[DeCiccio, Charles]. *The City College: Celebrating 125 Years of Free Higher Education*. New York: City College of the City University of New York, 1972.

Delson, Sandra. "Leadership in a Public Institution of Higher Education during a Period of Declining Enrollment and Declining Resources [Queens College]." Ph.D. diss., Columbia University Teachers College, 1986.

Demetriou, Sophia. "Rethinking Co-op—a Model for Change [Queens College]." *Journal of Cooperative Education* 30 (Winter 1995):34–38.

Draper, Hal. "The Student Movement of the Thirties." In *As We Saw the Thirties: Essays on Social and Political Movements of a Decade*, edited by Rita James Simon. Urbana: University of Illinois Press, 1967.

Dunlap, Barbara J. "Games of Champions, Games of Enthusiasts." *Alumnus* [*City College*] 92 (Summer 1997): 12–13.

Dyer, Conrad. "Protest and the Politics of Open Admissions: The Impact of the Black and Puerto Rican Students' Community [of City College]." Ph.D. diss., City University of New York, 1990.

Ergstrom, Kristina Dawn. "Radical or Respectable? Class and Ethnicity in the Early Student Peace Movement at Hunter College, 1932–1935." M.A. thesis, Sarah Lawrence College, 1995.

Eurich, Alvin C. "New York State Plans Community Colleges." *Education Digest* 15 (April 1950):48–49.

Evans, Sarah M. *Born for Liberty: A History of Women in America*. New York: The Free Press, 1989.

"Experiment at 292 Convent Avenue." *City College Alumnus* 32 (1936):73, 77.

Farmer, Martha. "Background Objectives and Program of the Division of Student Activities, School of General Studies, the City College of New York." Ph.D. diss., Columbia University, 1956.

Fields, Ralph R. *The Community College Movement*. New York: McGraw-Hill, 1962.

Finley, John Huston. "Address by President Finley [at dedication of new college buildings]." *City College Quarterly* 4 (1908):93–95.

Fischel, Jack Robert. "Harry Gideonse: the Public Life." Ph.D. diss., University of Delaware, 1973.

Fischler, Stan. *The Subway: A Trip Through Time on New York's Rapid Transit*. New York: H & M Productions II Inc., 1997.

"Forty Years of House Plan." *City College Alumnus* 69 (February 1974):5–8.

Freedman, Morris. "I Teach at CCNY." *Virginia Quarterly Review* 59 (Summer 1983): 498–515.

Frommer, Harvey. *City Tech: the First 40 Years*. Brooklyn, N.Y.:Technical College Press, 1986.

Frusciano, Thomas J, and Marilyn H. Pettit. *New York University and the City: An Illustrated History*. With a foreword by L. Jay Oliva. New Brunswick, N.J.: Rutgers University Press, 1997.

Gall, Lenore Rosalie. "The Core Curriculum at Brooklyn College: The Faculty Describes Its Impact." Ph.D. diss., Columbia University Teachers College, 1988.

Gilman, Cherni L. "Subverting Fiscal Crisis: A Case Study of a Public Educational Organization's Successful Fight for Survival [John Jay College]." Ph.D. diss., New York University, 1987.

Glazer, Nathan. "The College and the City Then and Now: Address [City College]." *The Public Interest* (Summer 1998):30–44.

———. "Facing Three Ways: City and University in New York Since World War II." In *The University and the City: from Medieval Origins to the Present*, edited by Thomas Bender, 267–89. New York: Oxford University Press, 1998.

Goldberger, Edward. "Twenty-five Years of House Plan." *City College Alumnus* 55 (October 1959):11–13.

Golway, Terry. *LaGuardia Community College: the First 25 Years*. Long Island City, N.Y.: LaGuardia Community College of the City University of New York, 1997.

Gordon, Sheila. "The Transformation of the City University of New York, 1945–1970." Ph.D. diss., Columbia University Teachers College, 1975.

Gordy, J. P. *Rise and Growth of the Normal School Idea in the United States*. Washington: Government Printing Office, Bureau of Education Circular of Information, No. 8, 1891.

Gorelick, Sherry. *City College and the Jewish Poor: Education in New York 1880–1924*. New Brunswick, N.J.: Rutgers University Press, 1981.

Gornick, Vivian. "Commencement Address." In *City at the Center*, edited by Betty Rizzo and Barry Wallenstein, 83–86. New York: Division of Humanities, City College of the City University of New York, 1983.

Graham, Patricia. "Expansion and Exclusion: A History of Women in American Higher Education." *Signs* 3 (Summer 1978):750–73.

Griffen, Alice. "New Look on the Bronx Campus." *King Kade* (c. 1959).

Gross, Theodore. *Academic Turmoil: the Reality and Promise of Open Admissions*. Garden City, N.Y.: Anchor Press/Doubleday, 1980.

Grunfeld, Katherina Koo. "Behold the People's College: 1870–1895." *Echo* (1995): 5–16.

———. "Purpose and Ambiguity: the Feminine World of Hunter College, 1869–1945." Ph.D. diss., Fordham University, 1991.

Heller, Louis. *Death of the American University with Special Reference to the Collapse of City College of New York*. New Rochelle, N.Y.: Arlington House, 1973.

Hermalyn, Gary. *Morris High School and the Creation of the New York City Public High School System*. Bronx, N.Y.: Bronx Historical Society, 1995.

[Hillel, Halkin] "Menorah Association and *Menorah Journal*." In *Encyclopaedia Judaica*. New York: Macmillan Company, 1971.

"Hispanics, Higher Education's Missing People." *Change* 28 (May/June 1988):4, 6–10+.

Hood, Clifton. *733 Miles: The Building of the Subways and How They Transformed New York*. Baltimore: The Johns Hopkins University Press, 1993.

Horowitz, Helen Lefkowitz. *College Life: Undergraduate Cultures from the End of the Eighteenth Century to the Present*. Chicago: The University of Chicago Press, 1986.

Horowitz, Murray M. *Brooklyn College, the First Half Century*. New York: Brooklyn College Press, 1981.

Howe, Irving. *A Margin of Hope: An Intellectual Autobiography*. San Diego: Harcourt Brace Javanovich, 1982.

Jackson, Kenneth T., ed. *The Encyclopedia of New York City*. New Haven: Yale University Press, 1995.

Jordan, David Starr. "The Question of Coeducation." *Munsey's Magazine* 34 (1906):684.

Karrp, Mortimer. "The House Plan." *City College Alumnus* 31 (1935):74–75.

Katzenstein, Herbert. "Private and Social Benefits of the College Degree in Black Males, 1962–1970: A Sample of Graduates of the City College of New York and Howard University." Ph.D. diss., City University of New York, 1972.

Keefer, Louis E. *Scholars in Foxholes: The Story of the Army*

Specialized Training Program in World War II. Jefferson, N.C.: McFarland & Company, 1988.

Kerr, Bette. "Goals of Hostos Community College as Perceived by Its Constituent Groups." Ph.D. diss., Fordham University, 1981.

[Klapper, Paul]. "Courses for Teachers, Librarians and Social Workers." *City College Quarterly* 17 (March 1921):3–11.

Kovar, Lillian Cohen. *Here to Complete Dr. King's Dream: The Triumphs and Failures of a Community College*. Lanham, Md.: University Press of America, 1996.

Kreuzer, James R. *Lehman College: a Look Back, a Look Ahead*. Bronx, N.Y.: Herbert H. Lehman College of the City University of New York, [1968]. Herbert H. Lehman Memorial Lecture, 1968.

Kriegel, Leonard. "Expendable CUNY: End of a Free University." *New Republic* 75 (October 2, 1976):3–11.

———. *Working Through: A Teacher's Journey in the Urban University*. New York: Saturday Review Press, 1972.

Kristol, Irving. "Memoirs of a Trotskyite." In his *Neoconservatives: The Autobiography of an Idea*, 469–80. New York: The Free Press, 1995.

Lavin, David E. *Access to Higher Education: Institutional Responses to Open Admissions at the City University of New York*. New York: City University of New York, 1976.

Lavin, David E., Richard D. Alba, and Richard Silberstein. *Right Versus Privilege: the Open Admissions Experiment of the City University of New York*. New York: The Free Press, 1981.

Lavin, David E., and David Hyllegard. *Changing the Odds: Open Admissions and the Life Chances of the Disadvantaged*. New Haven: Yale University Press, 1996.

Levine, Arthur, and Deborah Hirsch. "Making a Meaningful Impact." *Change* 28 (May/June 1988):48–53.

Love, Robert A. "New Friends for City College." *City College Alumnus* 43 (December 1947):8–9.

Markowitz, Gerald E. *Education for Justice: A Brief History of the John Jay College of Criminal Justice*. New York: John Jay College Press, 1990.

Marshak, Robert Eugene. *Academic Renewal in the 1970s: Memoirs of a City College President*. Washington, D.C.: University Press of America, 1982.

Marshall, L. C. "The American Collegiate School of Business." In *The Collegiate School of Business: Its Status at the Close of the First Quarter of the Twentieth Century*, edited by L. C. Marshall, 3–44. Chicago: University of Chicago Press, 1928.

Mayhew, Ira. *The Means and Ends of Universal Education*. New York: A. S. Barnes & Co., 1867.

McCabe, Helen Marie. "Cooperative Education in the Community College: A Critical Analysis." Ph.D. diss., Columbia University Teachers College, 1980.

Midgley, Simon. "Rich Tradition of America's 'Poor University'." *Times (London) Educational Supplement* (23 May 1980):10.

Minutes of the Board of Trustees of the College of the City of New York. New York: The Board, 1870–1926.

Morales, Thomas. "A Comparison of the Undergraduates in Good Academic Standing Who Persist and Who Depart in the City College of New York." Ph.D. diss., State University of New York at Albany, 1998.

Mosenthal, Philip J., and Charles F. Horne, eds. *The City College: Memories of Sixty Years*. New York and London: G. P. Putnam's Sons, 1907.

Muller, Gilbert H. "Gateway to Success: Urban Community Colleges and Administrative Diversity." *New Directions in Community Colleges* 24 (Summer 1996):51–56.

Murphy, Joseph S. "The Public Urban University and Costs of Equality." *Proceedings of the Academy of Political Science* 35 (1983):14–22.

Murtha, James. *Persistence and Achievement: The June 1981 Graduates from the City University of New York*. New York: Office of the Deputy Chancellor, Institutional Research and Analysis, City University of New York, 1983.

Nadler, Harry C. "The Community College and the Technical Challenge: An Administrative Study of the Need and Development of Queensborough Community College." Ph.D. diss., New York University, 1963.

Neumann, Florence Margaret. "Access to Free Public Higher Education in New York City: 1847–1961." Ph.D. diss., City University of New York, 1984.

Nevins, Allan. *"Evening Post": A Century of Journalism*. New York: Boni & Liveright, 1922.

New York (State). Legislature. Joint Committee on the State Education System. *Report of the New York City Sub-Committee . . . Relative to the Public Educational System of the City of New York. Report of a Survey of the Colleges under the Control of the Board of Higher Education of the City of New York.* George D. Strayer, Director. [Albany: 1944] Legislative Document No. 60, 1944.

New York (N.Y.). Board of Education. *Report of the Select Committee Appointed to Inquire into the Application of That Part of the Literature Fund Which Is Apportioned by the Regents of the University of the City and County of New York*. New York: G. F. Nesbit, Stationer and Printer, 1847.

New York (N.Y.). Board of Higher Education. *1964 Master Plan for the City University of New York. Second Interim Revision*. New York: The Board, 1966.

New York (N.Y.). Board of Higher Education. *Minutes of Proceedings*. New York: Board of Higher Education, 1926/27–1979.

New York (N.Y.). Mayor's Committee on Management Survey. Education Management Study. *Administrative Management of the School System of New York City: Report of the Survey of the Board of Education and the Board of Higher Education*. 3 vols. George D. Strayer and Louis E. Yavner, directors. [New York, N.Y.: The Committee], 1951.

Page, Charles Hunt. *Fifty Years in the Sociological Enterprise: A Lucky Journey*. Amherst: University of Massachusetts Press, 1982.

Pardue, Duncan B., and Suzanne P. Ryder. *A Forty-Six Year Summary of the Board of Higher Education of the City of New York*. [New York]: Office of the Chancellor of the Board of Higher Education, 1973.

Parisi, Barbara. "The History of Brooklyn's Three Main Performing Arts Centers: The Brooklyn Academy of Music, Brooklyn Center for the Performing Arts at Brooklyn College and St. Ann's Center for the Restoration of the Arts, Inc." Ph.D. diss., New York University, 1991.

Patterson, Samuel White. *Hunter College: Eighty-Five Years of Service*. New York: Lantern Press, 1955.

Pearson, Paul David. *The City College of New York: 150 Years of Academic Architecture*. New York: The City College of the City University of New York, 1997.

Phelps-Stokes, Isaac Newton. *The Iconography of Manhattan Island 1498–1909*. 6 vols. New York: H. Dodd, 1915–1928.

Podell, Lawrence. *City University Student Survey*. New York: Office of Program Policy Research, City University of New York, 1977.

Pomerantz, Sidney I. "New York in the Year 1847." *City College Alumnus* 42 (October 1946):93–107.

Poremski, Karen M. "CUNY-Bernard M. Baruch College: Philanthropy in American Culture." *Liberal Education* 74 (September/October 1988):30–31.

Powell, Colin L. (with Joseph E. Pergico), *My American Journey*. New York: Random House, 1995.

Preminger, Alex, Antoinette Ciolli, and Lillian Lester. *Urban Educator: Harry D. Gideonese, Brooklyn College and the City University of New York: An Annotated Bibliography*. New York: Twayne Publishers, 1970.

Programme of the Installation of John H. Finley. New York: College of the City of New York, 1903.

Ragsdale, George T. "The Police Training School." *Annals of the American Academy of Political Science* 146 (November 1929):170–76.

Reyes, Florida. "The Effects of Peer Counseling on the Academic Performance of College Students in a Predominantly Minority Institution [Medgar Evers College]." Ph.D. diss., Columbia University Teachers College, 1981.

"Richard Rogers Bowker '68." *City College Alumnus* 30 (January 1934):5–9.

Rodriguez-Fraticelli, Carlos. "Hostos Community College and the Puerto Rican Struggle for Equity in Education." *Centro* 2 (1987–1988):23–32.

Rosenthal, Irving. "A History of Student Publications at the College of the City of New York." M.S. in Education thesis, College of the City of New York, 1934.

Ross, David R. B. "Herbert H. Lehman College." *The Bronx County Historical Society Journal* 16 (Fall 1979):91–100.

———. *Herbert H. Lehman College of the City University of New York*. New York, (s.n.), 1979.

Rossman, Jack E. *Open Admissions at City University of New York: An Analysis of the First Year.* Englewood Cliffs, N.J.: Prentice-Hall, 1975.

Rudy, Solomon Willis. *The College of the City of New York: A History, 1847–1947. A Centennial History.* New York: City College Press, 1949.

Savage, Arthur. *Report to the Board of Higher Education of the City of New York with Respect to Its Bylaws and Procedures in Relation to Student Due Process.* New York: Gasparini, Koch and Savage, 1968.

Scelsa, Joseph U. "The 80th Street Mafia." In *Beyond the Godfather*, 289–306. Edited by A. Kenneth Ciongoli and Jay Parini. Amherst: University Press of New England, 1997.

Schappes, Morris U. "On Immigrant Education—Then and Now." *City College Alumnus* 82 (June 1987):7–8+.

Semi-Annual Report of the President of the Normal College for the Term Ending June 27, 1871. New York: The New York Printing Company, 1871.

Sinclair, Upton. *The Goose-Step: A Study of American Education.* Rev. ed. Pasadena, Calif: The Author, 1923.

Smith-Rosenberg, Caroll. *Disorderly Conduct: Visions of Gender in Victorian America.* New York: Alfred A. Knopf, 1985.

Solomon, Barbara Miller. *In the Company of Educated Women: A History of Women in Higher Education in America.* New Haven: Yale University Press, 1985.

Stepanchev, Stephen, ed. *People's College on the Hill: Fifty Years at Queens College 1937–1987.* New York: Queens College of the City University of New York, 1988.

Stolnitz, Jerome. *Lehman College: The Imperative of Change.* Bronx, N.Y.: Herbert H. Lehman College of the City University of New York, [1969]. Herbert H. Lehman Memorial Lecture, 1969.

Taft, Arthur. "One Hundred and Fifty Years of Sports at City College." *City College Alumnus* 68 (June 1973):9–17.

Tepsic, M. Jean. "Bread and Tickets: An Historical Study of the Dance Events at Lewisohn Stadium, 1925–1945." Ph.D. diss., New York University, 1994.

Traub, James. *City on a Hill: The American Dream at City College.* Reading, Mass.: Addison-Wesley Co., 1994.

Twentieth Annual Report of the Normal College for the Year Ending December 31, 1890, to which is appended a catalogue of the students, together with the class standing of each student. New York: Press of DeLeeuw and Oppenheimer, 1891.

United States Naval Training School (WR). *Navy Service: A Short History of the United States Naval Training School (WR), Bronx, N.Y.*, compiled by the Public Relations Office, U.S.N.T.S. (WR). Bronx, N.Y.: The School, [1945?].

University of the State of New York. *1969 Progress Report of the Board of Regents on the Regents' Statewide Plan for the Expansion and Development of Higher Education.* Albany: University of the State of New York: State Education Department, 1969.

Untermeyer, Sophie Guggenheimer. *Mother Is Minnie.* Garden City, N.Y.: Doubleday, 1960.

"An Urban University and the City." *Social Policy* 17 (Summer 1996):19–32.

Valentine, David T. *Manual of the Corporation of the City of New York for the Year 1847.* New York: Casper C. Childs, Printer, 1847.

Watson, Gladys (Hipple). *The Brooklyn College Student: A Pilgrim's Progress.* New York: Twayne Publishers, 1966.

Wechsler, James. *Revolt on the Campus.* New York: Covici-Freide, 1935.

Wein, Robert. "Women's College's and Domesticity 1875–1918." *History of Education Quarterly* 14 (Spring 1974):31–47.

Women's City Club of New York, Inc. *The Privileged Many: A Study of the City University of New York's Open Admissions Policy, 1970–1975.* New York: Women's City Club of New York, 1975.

Zerneck, Richard. "The Sporting Life at City." *City College Alumnus* 78 (June 1983): 11–15, 23.

Websites and Addresses of CUNY Colleges

http://www.baruch.cuny.edu
Bernard M. Baruch College
17 Lexington Avenue
New York, N.Y. 10010

http://www.bmcc.cuny.edu
Borough of Manhattan Community College
199 Chambers Street
New York, N.Y. 10007

http://www.bcc.cuny.edu
Bronx Community College
University Avenue and West 181st Street
Bronx, N.Y. 10453

http://www.brooklyn.cuny.edu
Brooklyn College
2900 Bedford Avenue
Brooklyn, N.Y. 10012

http://www.cuny.edu
City University of New York Central Office
535 East 80th Street
New York, N.Y. 10012

http://www.ccny.cuny.edu
City College
Convent Avenue at 138th Street
New York, N.Y. 10031

http://www.law.cuny.edu
CUNY Law School at Queens College
65-21 Main Street
Flushing, N.Y. 11367

http://www.mec.cuny.edu
Medgar Evers College
1650 Bedford Avenue
Brooklyn, N.Y. 11225

http://gc.cuny.edu
City University Graduate School and University Center
5th Avenue and 34th Street
New York, New York 10016

http://www.hostos.cuny.edu
Eugenio Maria de Hostos Community College
475 Grand Concourse
Bronx, N.Y. 10451

http://www.hunter.cuny.edu
Hunter College
695 Park Avenue
New York, N.Y. 10021

http://jjay.cuny.edu
John Jay College of Criminal Justice
899 10th Avenue
New York, N.Y. 10019

Websites and Addresses of CUNY Colleges

http://www.kbcc.cuny.edu
Kingsborough Community College
2001 Oriental Boulevard
Manhattan Beach
Brooklyn, N.Y. 11235

http://www.lagcc.cuny.edu
Fiorello LaGuardia Community College
31-10 Thompson Avenue
Long Island City, N.Y. 11101

http://www.lehman.cuny.edu
Lehman College
250 Bedford Park Boulevard West
Bronx, N.Y. 10468-1589

http://www.nyctc.cuny.edu
New York City Technical College
300 Jay Street
New York, N.Y. 11201

http://www.qc.cuny.edu
Queens College
Long Island Expressway and Kissena Boulevard
Flushing, N.Y. 11367

http://www.qcc.cuny.edu
Queensborough Community College
56th Avenue and Springfield Boulevard
Bayside, N.Y. 11364

http://www.csi.cuny.edu
York College
94-20 Guy R. Brewer Boulevard
Jamaica, N.Y. 11451

http://www.med.cuny.edu
Sophie Davis School of Biomedical Education/CUNY
Medical School
Robert E. Marshak Science Building
City College
Convent Avenue and 138th Street
New York, N.Y. 10031

A Sampling of CUNY Alumni

Irwin Shaw	1934	Henry Roth	1928	Evan Hunter	
Sam Levenson	1934	Zero Mostel	1935	(Ed McBain)	1950
Paule Marshall	1953	Bernard Malamud	1936	Gertrude Elion	1937
Lawrence Zicklin	1957	Irving Howe	1940	Lloyd Schwartz	1961
George Weissman	1939	Nathan Glazer	1944	Paul Mazursky	1957
William Newman	1947	Faith Ringgold	1955	Thomas Tam	1968
Bernard L. Schwartz	1948	Judd Hirsh	1960	Vivian Gornick	1957
Stan Ross	1956	Mario Runco	1974	Carlos Hernandez	1971
Sidney Harman	1939	Jonas Salk	1934	Susan Gubar	1965
Irwin Engelman	1955	Judith Crist	1941	Oscar Hijeuldos	1975
Sidney Mishkin	1934	Ada Louise Huxtable	1941	Hazelle Goodman	1986
Irving Weinstein	1923	Ruby Dee	1945	Daniel Goldin	1962
Bernard Baruch	1889	Shirley Chisholm	1946	Jane Tillman Irving	1959
Matthew Goldstein	1963	Frank Field	1947	Morris R. Cohen	1900
Claire Mason	1940	Earl Ubell	1948	Kenneth Arrow	1940
Eli Mason	1940	Stanley Cohen	1943	Herbert Hauptman	1937
Cleveland Abbe	1857	Herman Badillo	1951	Jerome Karle	1937
Evander Childs	1861	Edwin Torres	1955	Arthur Kornberg	1937
Richard Rogers Bowker	1868	Alan Dershowitz	1958	Rosalyn Yalow	1941
Frank Damrosch	1879	Sandra Feldman	1960	Leon Lederman	1943
George S. Davis	1880	Marvin Hamlisch	1967	Arnold Penzias	1955
Upton Sinclair	1897	Jerry Seinfeld	1976	Julius Axelrod	1933
Robert F. Wagner	1898	Juliet Papa	1978	Robert Hofstadter	1935
Felix Frankfurter	1902	Jimmy Smits	1980	Alfred Kazin	1935
Sam Jaffe	1912	Gloria Naylor	1981	John Johnson	1961
Edward G. Robinson	1914	Barbara Boxer	1962	A. Phillip Randolph	1919
Lewis Mumford	1916	Carl Spievogel	1952	Daniel Schorr	1938
Sidney Hook	1923	Stanley Kaplan	1939	Bernie West	1939

Index

Page numbers printed in *italics* refer to illustrations and/or annotations.

Abbe, Robert, 12
Accounting Forum (Baruch College), 74, 75
Admissions: during nineteenth century, 8–10; 1890s–1950s, 117–118; innovations during 1930s, 45; space considerations and, 118–120; from 1970, 120–122, 127
African Americans, 16, 50, 113, 120–121, 126
"Alcoves" (City College), *64*, 65
Alumni/nae, 141
American Student Union, 84
Anderson, Marian, at Lewisohn Stadium, *20*
Andreadis, George, 105
Archery, *105*
Army Specialized Training Program (ASTP), 89, *92*
Arrow (Hunter College), 74
Athletics, 97–110. *See also* Names of individual sports
Aurora (Queensborough Community College), 72

Babel (LaGuardia Community College), 77
Baruch, Bernard M., *52*, 45, *115*
Baruch (Bernard M.) School of Business and Public Administration. *See* School of Business (City College)
Baruch College, 115, 117. *See also* School of Business (City College)

Baseball, 98
Baskerville, Charles, 75
Baskerville Chemical Journal (City College), 75
Basketball, *101*, *103:* "Normal Five," *110*
Beecher, Catherine, 22
Bildersee, Adele, 62
Black and Puerto Rican Student Coalition, *120–121*
Board of Education (New York City), 2–3
Board of Higher Education (New York City): established, 38; and *Strayer Report*, 111, Committee to Look to the Future (1962), 112–113; master plan for City University of New York (1966), 119–120. *See also* Admissions; Tuition
Board of Trustees (City University of New York), 125, 127
Borough of Manhattan Community College, 63, *114*
Bosworth, Joseph S., 4
Bowker, Albert H., *113*, 120
Bowker, Richard Rogers, 16, *58*, 72–73
Boxing, *102*
Bridge (LaGuardia Community College), 77
Borough of Manhattan Community College, 63, *114*
Broeklundia (Brooklyn College), 72
Bronx Community College, 48, 50, *51*, 126
Brooklyn (Borough of): College proposed for, 36

Brooklyn College, 40, *41*, 45, 48, 62
Brunner, Arnold, *20*
Burchard, Lewis Sayre, *14*
Business education, 27, 38–40
Butler, Nicholas Murray, 36

Calling Card (Brooklyn College), 60
Campus (City College), 73
Carnegie Hall, 11,
Cavallaro, Joseph, 48
Chimento, Joseph, 90
Churchill, Thomas, 38
City College: 12–21: attacks on, 10, 13; moves to St. Nicholas Heights, 13, 16, *18*; buildings, *18*, *21*; public school teachers and, 34; Bronx Center, 46; Brooklyn Center, 40; Queens Center, 46. *See also* Admissions; Evening sessions; Free Academy; School of Business (City College); School of...; Tuition; Women
CCNY. *See* City College
City College of New York. *See* City College
City College Accountant (School of Business), 74
CUNY. *See* City University of New York
City University of New York (CUNY): created, 111–112; growth in 1960s–1970s, 115–119; facilities, 111, 117, 122; funding of, 125; remedial work at, 122, 125–127. *See also* Admissions; Tuition

City University of New York Athletic Conference, 109, *110*
City University of New York Construction Fund, 122
Civil War, 79–80
Class dinners, *59*
Clionia (Free Academy), 54, *55*, 56
Coeducation. *See* Women
Colden, Charles S., 46
"College Now," 128
College of Staten Island, 123. *See also* Staten Island Community College
College of the City of New York. *See* City College
College Preparatory Initiative, 127
Collegian, 58, 72–73
Columbia College, 2, 4
Commencements: during nineteenth century, *10–11, 25, 27*; at Lewisohn Stadium, 11, *21*; Queens College, first, 47
Community college movement, 47–48
Compton, Alfred G., 8, *14*, 79
Cone, Helen Gray, *29*, 33, *84*
Cooperative education, 116, 118
Cooperative Times (LaGuardia Community College), 77
Cottrell, Donald E., 115
Courier and Enquirer, 4
Criminal Justice Ethics (John Jay College), 117

Dana, Charles A., 10
Davis, George Samler, 29
Dickinson, Asa Don, 90
Doctoral programs. *See* Graduate School
Dolan, John, *107*
Dole, Robert: returns to Brooklyn College, *92*
Dollars and Sense (Baruch College), 75
Doremus, Robert Ogden, 15
Dormitory Authority of the State of New York (DASNY), 122
Doscher, Robert, *102*
Draper, John, 15

Echo (Hunter College), 31, *70*

Encounter (Baruch College), 75
English as a Second Language (ESL), 115, 127
Envoy (Hunter College), 74
Evening sessions, 27, 36, *37*, 44, *45*, 60
Evers, Medgar Wiley, 119

Female Normal and High School. *See* Hunter College
Fencing, *106*
Finley, John H., 16, *17*, 19, 73, 101
Fiorello's Flute (LaGuardia Community College), 77
Fire Science Review (John Jay College), 117
Fiterman, Miles, 114
Fiterman, Shirley, 114
"Five Demands," *120–121*. *See also* Admissions
Fonda, Jane, *95*
Football, 99, 102, *104*
Frankfurter, Felix, 55
Fraternities and secret societies, 56–57, 59, 63
Free Academy: established, 2–6; building, *5, 6, 7, 15, 39–40*; "burial of," *12*; curriculum at, 3, 6, 8, 10; discipline at, 8; grading at, 9. *See also* City College
Free Academy Microcosm, 70. *See also* *Microcosm*
Free tuition. *See* Tuition
Frick, Carol, *107*
Friedman, Benny, *104*
Frontiers (City College), 86

Gallagher, Buell G., 120–121
Garfield, James A., 38
Gasmasks, 82
Gershwin, George, at Lewisohn Stadium, *20*
Gideonse, Harry, 67, 69, 88, 104–105
Gillet, Joseph, 30, *34*
"Good Ship Alma Mater" (Hunter College), *29*
Gottschall, Morton, 42
G.I. Bill of Rights, 92, 117

Graduate School (City University of New York, *112, 113*, 126
Grand Central Palace, 39–40
Great Hall (City College), *18, 81*
Greene, Howard, 7
Greene, William Hallett, *16*
Grout, Edward, 36
Guggenheimer, Minnie, *20*

Hackett, James K., 63
Hahn, Adelaide E., 74
Hall, Abraham Oakey, 24
Hall of Fame of Great Americans, 50, 78
Hardy, John, 7
Harris, Townsend, 2, *3*, 4–5, 9, 19
Hartt, James Main, *10*
Harvest (LaGuardia Community College), 77
Havemeyer, William, 26
Hear Our Voices (Medgar Evers College), 75
Hillel Foundation (B'nai Brith), 67
Hispanics, 113, 115, 121, 126
Holman, Nat, 101–102, *103*
Hostos Community College, 115
House Plan, 59–60, *61*, 63
Howe, Irving, *65*
Humanist (LaGuardia Community College), 77
Hunter College, 22–35: established as a Normal school, 23–24; buildings, 24, *26*, 29, 122; curriculum, 24, 26–27, *30*, 32; library, 33, *34*; status changed, 32–33; Bronx Center, 42, *43*, 44, 89, 115; Brooklyn Center, *40*; business education, 42. *See also* Lehman College; Women
Hunter College Alumnae Association, 28, 34
Hunter College Bulletin, 72, 74
Hunter, Thomas, 24, 27, *32*, 54, 56, *57*

Immigrants, 1, 66–67, 126
Jessup, Walter A., 47
John Jay College of Criminal Justice, 76, *117*. *See also* Police

Jordan, David Starr, 40

Karpp, Mortimer, 59
Kelly, Robert, 24
Ken (Brooklyn College), 75
King, James J., 19n7
Kingsborough Community College, 72, 128
Kingsman (Brooklyn College), 75
Klapper, Paul, 47
Klitgord, Otto, 49
Korean War, 92, *93*
Kovar, Lillian C., 126
Kristol, Irving, *64–66*
Krowl, Henry Kates, 9

Lacrosse, 99, *100*
LaGuardia Community College, 65, 77, 116
LaGuardia, Fiorello, 46–47
Landscape (Brooklyn College), 75
Lehman College, 115. *See also* Hunter College: Bronx Center
Lehman, Herbert H., 115
Lenox Hill Neighborhood Association, *28*, 33
Lewisohn Stadium (City College), 11, *20–21*
Lewisohn, Adolph, *20–21*
Lexicon (Baruch College), 72
Literary and debating societies, 31, 54, *55*, 56
Literature Fund (New York State), *4*, 19
Lyons, James J., 51

McKenzie, Findlay, 90
McKibbin, Gilbert Hunt, *79*, 80
Main Events (City College), 75
Manhattan League (Free Academy), 56
Medgar Evers College, 75, 117, *119*
Megathon (City College), 66
Meister, Morris, 48
Menorah Clubs, 67
Mercury (City College), 71, 73
Merington, Marguerite, *32*, 33
Merrill, Jenny, *32*, 33

Mestre, Aurelius E., *80*, 81
Mezes, Sidney E., 19, 81
Microcosm (City College), 71
Moss, James A., 117

National Collegiate Athletic Association, *103*, 109
National Invitational Tournament (Basketball), *103*
National Student League, 84
Newman Clubs, 66
New York City Community College, 66. *See also* New York Institute of Applied Arts and Sciences
New York City Technical College, 49: student life at, *60*, 61, 65, *66*; *Statement*, 72
New York Herald, 10
New York Institute of Applied Arts and Sciences, 48, *49*, *93*
New York Public Library, 45
New York Sun, 10
New York Times: John H. Finley becomes editor, *17*; City College graduates and, 73
New York University, 2
Night Call (Brooklyn College), 75
Normal College Alumnae Settlement House, *28*
Normal College Bulletin, 74
Normal College of the City of New York. *See* Hunter College
Normal schools, 23–24

Odyssey (Kingsborough Community College), 72
"Open Admissions." *See* Admissions

Partisan Review, 65
Pen (John Jay College), 76, *78*
Phi Beta Kappa, 58
Phillips, William, 65
Philomathean (Hunter College), 31, 56, *57*
Phoenix (Queens College), 75
Phoenix (Staten Island Community College), 75

Phrenocosmia (Free Academy), *16*, 54, *55*, 56
"Plain Truth", 4
Poje, Helmut, 105
Police (New York City), and college programs, 32–33, 44, *46*, 117
Post, George B., 13, *18*
Powell, Colin L., 96
Public School Society, 2
Puerto Ricans, *120–121*, 126
Pulse Quarterly, 76

Queen Bee (City College: Queens Center), 46
Queensborough Community College, 50, 63, 72, *127*
Queens College, 46, 47, 63, 66, 72, 109, *125*
Queens Quair (City College: Queens Center), 46

Radio stations, student run, 56, *69*
Rahlens, Eileen, 107
Rampart (Queens College), 75
Rees, Mina, *112–113*
Regents (New York State Board of), admissions goal for City University in 1975, 120
Reilly, Carlton H., 105
Renwick, James, Jr., *5*, 6
Requa, Emma, 33
Reserve Officers Training Corps (ROTC), 82, *85*, 95–96
Rice, Edith, 34
Richman, Julia, *35*
Richmond College, 123. *See also* College of Staten Island
Ringling Brothers and Barnum and Bailey Circus, *41*
Robinson, Lucius, 10
Robinson, Frederick B., 37–38, *46*, *85*, 86
Rockefeller, Nelson, 112, 121, 124
Roosevelt, Eleanor, visits House Plan, 61

Saxe, Emmanuel, 68
Schnell, Muriel L., 90

School of Architecture and Urban Planning (City College), 117, 126
School of Biomedical Education (Sophie Davis)/City University of New York Medical School, 126
School of Business (City College: established, 39, 40; women admitted, 42, 53; Intensive Business Training Institute, 44–45, 92; freshman orientation at, 68; becomes Baruch College, 115, 117
School of Engineering (City College), 8, 14, 78, 126
School of Law (City University of New York at Queens College), 125, 126
School of Library and Information Studies (Queens College), 126
School of Social Work (Hunter College), 126
Sentences and Stanzas (Baruch College), 75
Settlement work, 28
Shahn, Ben: and *Mercury* (City College), 71
Silhouette (Queens College), 72
Smith, Alfred E., 38
Smith, Joseph, 106
Soccer, l05, *107*
Social Problems Clubs, 86
Sororities, 57, 63
Spanish-American War, *80*, 81
Spanish civil war, 86
Spirit (York College), *78*
Spotlight (Brooklyn College), 74
State Literature Fund (New York), 4
Statement (New York City Technical College), 72
Staten Island (College of). *See* College of Staten Island

Staten Island Community College, 48, 75, 105, *107*
Steers, James Rich, 14
Strayer, George D., 111
Strayer Report 67–69, 111–112
Student Army Training Corps (SATC), 81
Student government, 58
Student life, 54–69: clubs, 65–67, 86, *96*; facilities for, 63, 67; hazing, 63; President J. Finley, attitude toward, *17*; President T. Hunter, attitude toward, *31*, 54, 56
Student Life (Departments of), 63, 68
Student protests and demonstrations: during the Depression, 82, 84, *86*, 87; during Vietnam era, *94*, *95*; "Five Demands" and, 120–121; free tuition, rallies to support, *124*
Student publications, 70–78. *See also* Individual titles
Swimming, 107,, *108*

Tead, Ordway, 44
Tennis, 107
Tilton, Theodore, 70
Townsend Harris Hall High School, 19, 39
Track and field, 107, *109*
Tuition: free tuition, heritage of, 6, 24, 111; legislative mandate for free tuition eliminated, 112; as source of student protest, 121, *124*; proposed, 122–123; first imposed, 125

United Nations, 89

Vanguard (Brooklyn College), 74
Vector (City College), 78

Veterans, 93–94
Vietnamese Conflict (1961–1975), 94, *95*

Wadleigh, Lydia, *32*, 33
Wadleigh Memorial Library Alcove, 33, *34*
Walker, James J., 40
WAVES, *89*, 90,
Webb, Alexander Stewart, 4, 6, *13*: curricular views of, *13*; defends City College, 10–11; obtains laboratory, *15*, student publications and, 71;
Webb, James Watson, 4, 6
Webster, Horace, *8*, 12, 56, 58, 127
West Point (U.S. Military Academy at), *8*, 12
White, Stanford, 50
Wilson, Margaret, 34
Wisterion (Hunter College), 70–71
Wolfe, Jack, *88*
Women: education of during nineteenth century, 22–24, 28; in evening sessions, *37*, 46, *60*; Brooklyn College and, 40: City College, admitted to programs at, 42, 44; secretarial training and, 42, *53*; during World War I, *83–84*; as student athletes, *101*, *103*, *105–106*, 107, *108*, *110*. *See also* Hunter College
Wood, William, *32*
World War I, 81–82, *83–84*, 85
World War II, 48, 83,88–92, *88–92*

York College, 78, 117, *118*
Young, John, 6
Young Men Christian Association (YMCA), 65